SpringerBriefs in Computer Science

Series editors

Stan Zdonik, Brown University, Providence, Rhode Island, USA
Shashi Shekhar, University of Minnesota, Minneapolis, Minnesota, USA
Xindong Wu, University of Vermont, Burlington, Vermont, USA
Lakhmi C. Jain, University of South Australia, Adelaide, South Australia, Australia
David Padua, University of Illinois Urbana-Champaign, Urbana, Illinois, USA
Xuemin Sherman Shen, University of Waterloo, Waterloo, Ontario, Canada
Borko Furht, Florida Atlantic University, Boca Raton, Florida, USA
V. S. Subrahmanian, University of Maryland, College Park, Maryland, USA
Martial Hebert, Carnegie Mellon University, Pittsburgh, Pennsylvania, USA
Katsushi Ikeuchi, University of Tokyo, Tokyo, Japan
Bruno Siciliano, Università di Napoli Federico II, Napoli, Italy
Sushil Jajodia, George Mason University, Fairfax, Virginia, USA
Newton Lee, Newton Lee Laboratories, LLC, Tujunga, California, USA

SpringerBriefs present concise summaries of cutting-edge research and practical applications across a wide spectrum of fields. Featuring compact volumes of 50 to 125 pages, the series covers a range of content from professional to academic.

Typical topics might include:

- A timely report of state-of-the art analytical techniques
- A bridge between new research results, as published in journal articles, and a contextual literature review
- A snapshot of a hot or emerging topic
- An in-depth case study or clinical example
- A presentation of core concepts that students must understand in order to make independent contributions

Briefs allow authors to present their ideas and readers to absorb them with minimal time investment. Briefs will be published as part of Springer's eBook collection, with millions of users worldwide. In addition, Briefs will be available for individual print and electronic purchase. Briefs are characterized by fast, global electronic dissemination, standard publishing contracts, easy-to-use manuscript preparation and formatting guidelines, and expedited production schedules. We aim for publication 8–12 weeks after acceptance. Both solicited and unsolicited manuscripts are considered for publication in this series.

More information about this series at http://www.springer.com/series/10028

Zhi Wang · Wenwu Zhu · Shiqiang Yang

Online Social Media Content Delivery

Delivery

A Data-Driven Approach

 Springer

Zhi Wang
Graduate School at Shenzhen
Tsinghua University
Shenzhen, China

Shiqiang Yang
Department of Computer Science
Tsinghua University
Beijing, China

Wenwu Zhu
Department of Computer Science
Tsinghua University
Beijing, China

ISSN 2191-5768   ISSN 2191-5776   (electronic)
SpringerBriefs in Computer Science
ISBN 978-981-10-2773-4   ISBN 978-981-10-2774-1   (eBook)
https://doi.org/10.1007/978-981-10-2774-1

Library of Congress Control Number: 2018947498

Printed on acid-free paper

This Springer imprint is published by the registered company Springer Nature Singapore Pte Ltd.
The registered company address is: 152 Beach Road, #21-01/04 Gateway East, Singapore 189721, Singapore

Preface

The delivery of online social video content has become an intriguing research area, along with the increasing popularity of online social networks. Traditional content delivery approaches that are designed without considering social topology and user behaviors are less efficient—if not completely ineffective—for social and socialized content delivery. To address the social video delivery problem, this book studies data-driven solutions, which jointly consider social relationship, user behavior, and content features. It focuses on the characteristics of user preferences in social media, network topology optimization and resource allocation for social content delivery, propagation-based social content replication, and social video service deployment.

1. **Joint Content- and Social-Based User Preference Mining.** The rapid growth of user-generated social videos requires content delivery systems to understand user preferences. To date, user preference inference for social video content has been studied separately: based on either content similarity or user relationships. We investigate a joint social content preference mining framework by using social factors and content factors to jointly learn which content a user will import or re-share in an online social network. In particular, we study a joint matrix completion framework. Experimental results demonstrate that the proposed approach substantially improves the preference mining relative to the baseline approaches.

2. **Enhancing Multimedia Network Resource Allocation Using Social Prediction.** Popularity patterns of social video content have greatly changed: video popularity is highly affected by online social networks, and videos can become 'viral' almost instantaneously. These changes make traditional popularity-based network resource allocation for video services suboptimal. It is intriguing to study a proactive network resource allocation strategy for social video services. Using influential factors summarized from measurement studies, we propose a learning-based framework that uses propagation parameters to predict the number of potential viewers and their geographic distribution. We present proactive strategies that determine the upload capacities of servers in

different regions. We also present experimental results that verify the effectiveness of the proposed algorithms.

3. **Propagation-Based Socially Aware Content Replication.** Online social networks have reshaped the manner in which content is generated, distributed, and consumed on today's Internet. It is intriguing to study service provision of social content for global users with satisfactory quality-of-experience. We conduct large-scale measurements of real-world online social networks to study social propagation and discover important propagation patterns, including social locality, geographical locality, and temporal locality. Motivated by the findings from the measurements, we propose a propagation-based socially aware content delivery framework that uses a hybrid edge-cloud and peer-assisted architecture. Replication strategies are further designed for the architecture based on three propagation predictors designed by jointly considering user, content, and context information. These findings and strategies change the prevalent method of content delivery, which is only based on content popularity, and significantly improve the user experience in receiving social content.

4. **Joint Online Processing and Geo-Distributed Delivery for Dynamic Social Streaming.** Adaptive social streaming has grown rapidly in popularity because it allows heterogeneous users to receive different bitrates. To date, the two important components in dynamic adaptive social streaming—video transcoding, which generates the adaptive bitrates for a video, and video delivery, which streams videos to users—have been separately studied, resulting in a significant waste of computation and storage resources due to transcoding unneeded video data and suboptimal streaming quality due to homogeneous video replication. We investigate the possibility of jointly performing video transcoding and video delivery for adaptive social streaming in an online manner according to the user preferences that are learned from their social behaviors and their preferences of edge servers to receive the video chunks. The proposal significantly improves both the user experience in adaptive social streaming and computational resources utilization of the system.

Shenzhen, China   Zhi Wang
Beijing, China   Wenwu Zhu
Beijing, China   Shiqiang Yang

Acknowledgements

We would like to express our gratitude to our colleagues, friends, and our families, who saw us through this book; to the editors and reviewers; and to all those who provided support and engaged in useful discussions.

Contents

Chapter 1
Introduction

Abstract In this chapter, we provide a review of online video content delivery, presenting the traditional video delivery approaches and the facing challenges. To satisfy the trend for content to be dynamically processed before being delivered to users, we propose a joint online processing and delivery paradigm to improve the user experience in social video services. At the end of this chapter, we give out the structure of the whole book.

Keywords Social media · Social content delivery · Social propagation

1.1 Background

Online social networks have become a popular online service, with an ever increasing number of social network apps, including ones based on "friend" relationships (e.g., Facebook), ones based on "following" relationships (e.g., Twitter), and ones based on professional connections (i.e., LinkedIn). Such applications have successfully changed the manner in which people are connected to each other. In an online social network, users receive a variety of multimedia content, of which online video services are important ones, dominating a large fraction of today's traffic.

Online social networks and online video services are closely connected to each other: users can "import" video content from video sharing sites to online social networks and share the videos with social connections. Such social behaviors have changed how content is delivered to users: using online social networks has become a normal method of accessing videos. Users' actions determine how people select videos to watch, changing the assumption of traditional content delivery systems that users can only *passively* receive content from a content provider.

Traditional video delivery has evolved in the following four stages:

Simple Client/Server (C/S): In this stage, there was little information delivered by the Internet. The number of users and amount of content were both very small. The traditional Client/Server mode uses limited server resources to serve a limited number of users.

© The Author(s) 2018

Z. Wang et al., *Online Social Media Content Delivery*,

SpringerBriefs in Computer Science, https://doi.org/10.1007/978-981-10-2774-1_1

IP Multicast: IP Multicast was proposed to scale the system when users and video content were both increasing, in the sense that the load of servers can be alleviated by multicasting networking infrastructure [4]. In IP multicast, video packets are duplicated by in-network routers and sent to dedicated destinations, such that routers assist in the content delivery.

Application-Layer Multicast (ALM): The requirement of a multicast infrastructure limited the large deployment of IP multicast for video streaming. An alternative of application-layer multicast was invented. By letting users cache the video *chunks* they have downloaded and serve each other, application-layer multicast alleviates the load of streaming servers [2].

Content Delivery Network (CDN): In application-layer multicast, because video packets are delivered by individual peers joining and leaving the system on their own, the quality of content delivery is not guaranteed. Moreover, applications that use application-layer multicast schemes usually require users to install third-party software or plugins to enable the overlay content delivery. To address these problems, CDN-based video streaming has been proposed such that users can receive video chunks using their browsers via HTTP.

To summarize, traditional video delivery strategies are mainly based on ideas to redesign and improve the network to address the demands imposed by an increasing number of users. Today, online social networks and online video services have been cross-pollinating, e.g., Facebook allows users to upload and share videos, and YouTube has started to incorporate social connections from Google Plus. Such new trends make the two types of services influence each other. For example, the online video clip "Gangnam Style" has attracted more than 1 billion views since its publication owing to its propagation over popular online social network services, including Twitter and Facebook. Traditional video delivery, in which passive content delivery strategies are generally adopted, is facing fundamental challenges.

Traditional content delivery strategies that are based only on the awareness of passive content access are not able to proactively predict how individuals influence each other. Thus, we study video content delivery strategies that can satisfy the diverse geographical distribution of users, the dynamical network resource at different regions, the influence of social connections and user behaviors.

1.2 Research Challenges

Data-driven social content delivery is facing the following challenges:

System scalability in the UGC (user-generated content) era. The first challenge is due to the massive amount of video content generated by users in online social networks. In 2013, YouTube reported that more than 100 hours of video clips were uploaded by users in every minute. The amount of user-generated videos is much greater than that generated by conventional content providers. The trend of user-generated content has challenged traditional video delivery strategies as follows:

(1) traditional video delivery strategies only study how content can be effectively delivered to users, not how content can be efficiently uploaded by users. (2) The popularity distribution in an UGC system is different from that in a traditional online video sharing system, and new content caching strategies are in demand. (3) Online social video service is serving users all over the world, who have diverse "preferences" for different edge server resources (e.g., a user wants to download from a server nearby such that the download speed is high). This requires new content deployment strategies that are based on the global network infrastructure. How to design such strategies in the context that content propagates among users via social connections is a research challenge.

Edge Content Distribution: In online social networks, content is generated, propagated, and distributed at the edge of the network, which is different from the traditional manner in which central content providers produce content and distribute it to edge users. This change has challenged traditional content delivery as follows: (1) how videos are viewed and downloaded by users is no longer determined by any centralized agent, including online social network service providers, but rather affected by users' behaviors and social connections. Traditional content delivery strategies based on static patterns are not effective for delivering social video content that draws dynamical social attention. (2) Much unpopular content is shared among small social groups via online social video services. How to effectively distribute this content using limited edge server resources is a critical research problem. In this book, we study this problem from the aspects of user preferences and geographical distribution, which jointly yield a propagation-based network design for social video delivery.

Dynamical Content Propagation: Social propagation of content between social connections, which determine how content is finally viewed by users, is influenced by the topology of the social graph of people, user behaviors, and the content characteristics [5]. Propagation is fundamentally dynamical due to user behaviors. Traditional content delivery strategies tend to be network- and content-aware, but they are not user-aware, lacking the ability to proactively understand how a video content will propagate dynamically in online social networks.

Changed Popularity Distribution: Due to the large amount of user-generated content and the fact that content propagation is influenced by dynamical user behaviors, the popularity distribution of social video content has changed from a traditional power-law-like distribution to a complicated hybrid "flat-and-longtail" pattern. It is a challenge for traditional content delivery strategies to effectively treat such social video content, e.g., Mislove et al. observed that the request hit ratio degraded by more than 70% when traditional cache strategies were used to cache online social contents [3]. In this book, we study content delivery strategies that take this change in the popularity distribution of social video content into consideration.

Joint Content Delivery and Processing: Online social network services provide OpenAPIs for other online application/services to utilize the information including social relationship and user profiles [1]. Such a development paradigm has motivated a large number of social/socialized multimedia applications, in which a variety of content processing procedures have been invented, including content analysis and enhancement. In online social video applications, such content processing is also popular because video clips can be improved before being distributed to users. This trend also challenges traditional content delivery systems, which only act as "pipes" to deliver content to users without the power of processing content. To satisfy the trend for content to be dynamically processed before being delivered to users, we propose a joint online processing and delivery paradigm to improve the user experience in social video services.

1.3 Organization and Contributions

The organization of this book is as follows:

1. **Joint Content and Social Preference Mining**. Online social networks are emerging as a promising alternative for users to directly access video content. By allowing users to import videos and re-share them through the social connections, a large number of videos are available to users in online social networks. The rapid growth of user-generated videos provides enormous potential for users to find the ones that interest them, whereas the convergence of online social network services and online video sharing services makes it possible to make recommendations using social and content factors jointly. We design a joint social-content recommendation framework to suggest to users which videos to import or re-share via online social networks. In this framework, we first propose a user-content matrix update approach that updates and fills in cold user-video entries to provide the foundations for the recommendations. Then, based on the updated user-content matrix, we construct a joint social-content space to measure the relevance between users and videos, which can provide a high accuracy for video importing and re-sharing recommendations.

2. **Enhancing Multimedia Network Resource Allocation Using Social Prediction**. Online microblogging, where users follow other people that they are interested in and exchange information between themselves, has become very popular on today's Internet. Among these exchanges, video links are a representative type of content on a microblogging site. The impact is fundamental—not only do some viewers using a video service directly originate as a result of the microblog sharing and recommendation, but the users of microblogging sites also represent a promising sample of all viewers. It is intriguing to study a proactive service deployment for such videos using the propagation patterns of microblogs. Based on extensive traces from Youku and Tencent Weibo, a popular video sharing site and a top microblogging system, we explore how video propagation patterns in the microblogging system are correlated with video popularity on the video sharing site. Using influential factors summarized from the measurement studies, we further design a neural network-based learning framework to predict the number

of potential viewers and their geographic distribution. We then design proactive video deployment algorithms based on the prediction framework, which not only determines the upload capacities of servers in different regions but also strategically replicates videos to these regions to serve users.

3. **Propagation-Based Socially Aware Content Replication**. Online social networks have reshaped the manner in which multimedia content is generated, distributed and consumed on today's Internet. Given the massive amount of user-generated content shared via online social networks, users are moving to directly access this content via their preferred social network services. It is intriguing to study the service provision of social content for global users with satisfactory quality-of-experience. We conduct large-scale measurement using a real-world online social network system to study social content propagation. We have observed important propagation patterns, including social locality, geographical locality and temporal locality. Motivated by these measurement insights, we propose a propagation-based socially aware delivery framework that uses a hybrid edge-cloud and peer-assisted architecture. We also design replication strategies for the architecture based on three propagation predictors designed by jointly considering user, content and context information. In particular, we design a propagation region predictor and a global audience predictor to guide how the edge-cloud servers backup the content and a local audience predictor to guide how peers cache content for their friends.

4. **Joint Online Processing and Geo-distributed Delivery for Dynamic Social Streaming**. Dynamic adaptive video streaming has emerged as a popular approach for video streaming on today's Internet. To date, the two important components in dynamic adaptive streaming—video transcoding, which generates the adaptive bitrates of a video, and video delivery, which streams videos to users—have been separately studied, resulting in a significant waste of computational and storage resources due to transcoding useless videos and suboptimal streaming quality due to homogeneous video replication. We propose jointly performing video transcoding and video delivery for adaptive streaming in an online manner. We conduct extensive measurement studies of a video sharing system and a CDN to motivate our design. We formulate and solve optimization problems to enable high streaming quality for users and low computational and replication costs for the system. In particular, our design connects video transcoding and video delivery based on users' preferences for CDN regions and regional preferences for video versions.

References

1. http://open.qq.com
2. Y. Cui, B. Li, K. Nahrstedt, oStream: asynchronous streaming multicast in application-layer overlay networks. IEEE J. Sel. Areas Commun. **22**(1), 91–106 (2004)

3. A. Mislove, RethinkingWeb content distribution in the social media era, in *NSF Workshop on Social Networks and Mobility in the Cloud* (2012)
4. V. Thomas, White paper: IP multicast in RealSystem G2, in *RealNetworks, Inc* (1998)
5. Z. Wang et al., Cloud-based social application deployment using local processing and global distribution, in *ACM International Conference on emerging Networking EXperiments and Technologies (CoNEXT)* (2012)

Chapter 2
Joint Content- and Social-Based User Preference Mining

Abstract Understanding user preference is the key to efficient social content delivery, while user preference can be inferred from both content and social aspects in the context of online social content delivery. The chapter presents a general framework to understand user preference.

Keywords User preference · Recommendation · Social content recommendation

2.1 Introduction

Online social network services (e.g., Facebook and Twitter) and online video sharing service (e.g., YouTube) have emerged as the two most important services on today's Internet. The rapid convergence of the two services makes the market and industry of Internet Social TV very promising [7, 24, 28].[1] In the context of online social networks, video content is generated by individuals instead of centralized content providers [6], e.g., more than 60 h worth of videos are uploaded by users per minute on YouTube [36]. A large portion of the videos originally hosted on video sharing systems are "imported" by individuals to online social networks [32] and "re-shared" among users through social connections.

Online social networks are reshaping not only the manner in which videos are generated but also the manner in which users consume video content. The massive number of videos available makes it possible for users to directly find the videos that interest them in online social networks. In online social networks, users are willing to import and re-share videos [34]; however, it can be difficult for them to choose videos to import or re-share among the large number of videos available, making recommendations for both activities in demand. To realize the potential of such social video sharing, we are interested in recommendation of videos for the following two important social activities in online social networks [5]:

---

[1]©[2013] IEEE. Reprinted, with permission, from IEEE Transactions on Multimedia.

© The Author(s) 2018
Z. Wang et al., *Online Social Media Content Delivery*,
SpringerBriefs in Computer Science, https://doi.org/10.1007/978-981-10-2774-1_2

- *Importing recommendations* answers the question of "what videos to import?" In popular online social network systems such as Facebook and Twitter, most of the videos are not hosted by the social network systems. Instead, they are imported from other external video sharing systems; e.g., users can import videos from YouTube to Twitter by simply posting the links to the videos. The importing recommendation helps users discover interesting videos from video sharing websites.
- *Re-sharing recommendation* answers the question of "what videos to re-share?" After users have imported videos to an online social network, such videos are distributed through social connections; e.g., users on Twitter see the videos shared by people they follow and further re-share the videos to people who follow them, thus making the videos propagate in a cascading manner [18]. The re-sharing recommendation helps users discover the videos among the large number of videos shared by people that they follow.

Existing video recommendations include both *content-based recommendations* [25] and *social-based recommendations* [30]. In content-based recommendations, content-based filtering and collaborative filtering [27] have been widely studied. They are based on the content similarity from either content analysis or the users' historical ratings of content. Such recommendation approaches can provide a user with content similar to the content that he has viewed before or the content that users similar to him have viewed before, as illustrated in Fig. 2.1a. In contrast, in social-based recommendations, social relationships (e.g., friending and following) are used to filter the content distributed through the social connections, such that the content that one likes can be suggested to one's social connections [30]. Such a recommendation approach is able to provide users with content that has previously interested their friends, as illustrated in Fig. 2.1b.

In the context of online social networks, existing video recommendations are facing the following problems and challenges. (1) They lack a consideration of how content propagates through social connections, which is a unique feature of online social networks. (2) Importing and sharing videos in online social networks are implicit; i.e., users rarely give explicit ratings to videos they have imported/re-shared, which are required in many existing recommendation approaches. (3) Cold starts are even more challenging in the recommendation for today's user-generated contents

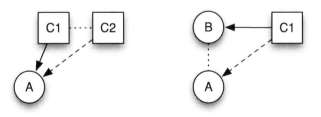

(a) Content-based recommendation.   (b) Social-based recommendation.

Fig. 2.1 Content-based recommendation and social-based recommendation

Fig. 2.2 Joint social and
content recommendation

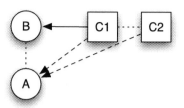

for two reasons. First, for users who have just joined the system, they have rarely
imported or shared videos in the system, thus making it difficult to recommend any
content for them, since existing recommendation systems rely on users' historical
preferences. Second, for videos imported by users who have few friends, a large
fraction of them have almost no viewers. It is difficult to determine the users to
whom such content should be recommended.

To address the above problems and challenges, we propose a joint social and content recommendation framework. Figure 2.2 illustrates the concept design, where
videos can be recommended to users according to both social relations and content
similarity. In particular, a *user-user matrix* (how users are socially connected), a
content-content matrix (how videos are similar to each other) and a *user-content
matrix* (how users import and re-share these videos) are utilized as inputs in our recommendation. More specifically, first, we propose a user-content matrix update algorithm by incorporating both social propagation and content similarity. We describe
how socially connected users influence each other and how similar videos can interest the same user, so as to predict which videos are to be imported/re-shared by
which users. In the update, entries for cold users and cold content in the user-content
matrix are updated and filled in to improve the recommendation. Second, based
on the updated user-content matrix, we build a joint *user-content space* to measure
the relevance between users and content. Dynamical adjustment of the weights of
user space and content space is employed to improve the recommendations for both
importing and re-sharing.

The remainder of this chapter is organized as follows. We summarize the related
works in Sect. 2.2. We introduce the framework of our recommendation method in
Sect. 2.3. We present the detailed recommendation algorithms in Sects. 2.4 and 2.5.
We discuss the efficiency issues and potential extensions of our recommendation
algorithms in Sect. 2.7. We evaluate the performance of our design in Sect. 2.6.

2.2 Related Work

In this section, we survey the literature regarding online social networks, video recommendation technologies, and recommendations in the context of online social
network.

2.2.1 Online Social Networks

Online social networks have become a popular research topic in recent years. Mislove et al. [23] use real world traces to study the topology of social graphs and confirm the power-law, small-world, and scale-free properties of online social networks. Krishnamurthy et al. [1] investigate Twitter and identify distinct classes of users and their behaviors, in addition to geographic growth patterns of the social network. Information in online social networks spreads among users in a "word-of-mouth" manner. A number of research efforts have been devoted to studying the propagation of information. Kwak et al. [20] investigate the impact of users' retweets on information diffusion in Twitter. Dodds et al. [10] use a contagion model to study information propagation, where a piece of information is considered an infective disease that spreads via social connections. Domingos et al. [11] explore the value of social networks in estimating the potential buyers of a product or a service, which can be influenced by an existing customer. Kempe et al. [18] investigate how to maximize the spread of influence in an online social network, and Hartline et al. [13] utilize the maximum spread to achieve revenue maximization. Recommendations in online social networks not only provide users with content that can interest them but also provide information that can potentially be used improve the service quality of the content sharing systems that host the socially distributed content [33].

In this chapter, we will explore the potential of using social propagation for user-generated video recommendation.

2.2.2 Social Recommendations

For general video recommendations, content collaboration and collaborative filtering have been widely used in the existing recommender systems [25, 27]. The basic idea is that when recommending content to a user, the content that is similar to the content that he has viewed before will be suggested. On the one hand, such similar content can be identified by content analysis methodologies; on the other hand, content that is accessed by similar users can also be considered similar. However, individually, these methods fail to provide good recommendations: (1) content-based approaches only measure the similarity using multimedia analysis, which cannot directly reflect users' interests, and (2) collaborative filtering suffers from the sparsity of users' preference databases [19].

Due to the above drawbacks of pure content-based and collaborative filtering approaches, some studies have combined the two to achieve better recommendation performance. Melville et al. [22] propose incorporating components from both content-based and collaboration filtering approaches to generate a hybrid recommender system, in which a content-based predictor is used to enhance the existing user data, where the pseudo user-ratings are generated based on the content analysis and used in the content-boosted collaborative filtering. Basilico et al. [3] design a kernel function between user-item pairs that allows simultaneous generalization across the user and item dimensions. There are also other recommendation frameworks for user-generated video recommendation. Baluja et al. [2] propose using a random walk through a co-view graph in YouTube to recommend videos.

In this chapter, we study how videos in online social networks can be suggested to users using the information from both online social networks and online video sharing networks.

2.2.3 Video Recommendation in the Context of Online Social Networks

Due to the large number of user-generated videos available in online social networks, recommendation is essential to realize the potential of social media in online social networks [37]. To keep users entertained and engaged, it is imperative that these recommendations are updated regularly and reflect a user's recent activity on the site [8]. Social connections and users' social activities are important records that can be used in video recommendations. Debnath et al. [9] propose improving the recommendation performance using online social networks, where the attributes used for content based recommendations are assigned weights depending on their importance to users. Walter et al. [30] propose a trust-based model to make recommendations, where users leverage their social connections to reach interesting information and make use of trust relationships to filter unwanted information. Since recommendation generally relies on users' private information (e.g., video ratings), it is challenging to perform content suggestion when users do not contribute their rating information. Isaacman et al. [16] have proposed to use matrix factorization for recommendations of user-generated content when the rating information is only shared between content producer and consumer pairs, which is a common privacy demand by users. Wang et al. [31] have studied recommendations for social groups using the followees' information of the users inside the groups instead of that of individuals in the online social network.

To the best of our knowledge, these is no study regarding using social propagation, content similarity analysis and users' social activities jointly to perform recommendations for user-generated videos. In this chapter, we explore how information from online social networks and online video sharing networks can be used jointly to improve the recommendation performance.

2.3 Framework

In this section, we first show the difference between importing recommendation and re-sharing recommendation; then, we present the framework for both types of recommendations.

2.3.1 Recommendation for Importing and Re-Sharing

Our recommendation is for users' imports and re-shares, i.e., we suggest videos that users might like to import to or re-share in an online social network. The two social activities are different as follows. (1) *Different purposes*. When importing videos to an online social network, users act as sources of video content, and they are willing to contribute videos that will interest their friends in the online social network. When re-sharing videos, they are helping the diffusion of the videos that are already in the online social network. (2) *Different scales*. In our measurement of Tencent Weibo, we observe that the number of imports by users is 6 times larger than the number of re-shares by users. People are more likely to generate videos than re-share videos that are already in Weibo. (3) *Different recommendation factors*. When importing a video, a user mainly considers the video itself, i.e., determines whether the video can interest his friends; when re-sharing a video, besides the video itself, the user also considers the user who shares the video in the first place, i.e., the user may be willing to help their friends to distribute a video. To perform recommendations for imports and re-shares, we first design a general recommendation model for both activities, then we suggest videos for imports and re-shares using different factors from the online social network and online content sharing network.

2.3.2 Recommendation Input: Matrices from Social Networks and Content Networks

We first introduce the information used in our design from both online social networks and online video sharing networks as follows: (1) a user matrix that represents how users follow each other in the online social network; (2) a content matrix that represents the similarity between the videos according to content analysis; and (3) an initial user-content matrix that represents how users import and re-share videos.

2.3.2.1 User-User Matrix

The microblogging system allows users to maintain "weak" social connections between each other, i.e., a user can generally follow anyone without their explicit permission. Thus, the social connections in a microblogging system can well reflect users' interests. From the technical team of Tencent Weibo, one of the largest microblogging systems in China [29], we have obtained traces recording how users are socially connected to each other. Let $\mathbf{A}$ denote the user-user matrix as follows:

$$\mathbf{A}_{ij} = \begin{cases} 1, & i \text{ follows } j, \text{ or } i = j \\ 0, & \text{otherwise} \end{cases} .$$

2.3.2.2 Content-Content Matrix

In traditional recommender systems, videos can be recommended only when they have been rated by some users before, i.e., after the system learns which users are interested in the videos [14, 15, 21, 26]. However, in an online social network, many user-generated videos are very cold and have almost no viewers. In our design, we perform recommendation for these videos by using content similarity analysis. In particular, we use a tag-based approach to construct the content similarity matrix as follows.

- *Collecting keywords from videos' tag lists.* The similarity between two videos is evaluated using the common keywords of their tags. The videos in Tencent Weibo are generally imported by users from other video sharing sites such as Youku, where each video i is given a list of tags before it is published, containing several short sentences describing content of the video. In our design, we first segment each sentence into several keywords in set W_i; then, we use the common keywords of two videos to evaluate their similarity.
- *Weighting the keywords.* One problem of the similarity calculation is the highly skewed frequency of the keywords, i.e., some keywords appear much more frequently than others. For example, the word "fun" is often chosen as a tag keyword. To resolve this problem, we adjust the weight of different keywords according to their appearance frequency. The weight z_w of a keyword w is defined as $z_w = \psi_1 + \psi_2 \frac{1}{P_w}$, where ψ_1, ψ_2 are two control parameters and P_w is the appearance frequency of w in all the videos. The rationale is that (1) if two videos have more common keywords, the similarity between them should be larger and (2) if a keyword is more common, the weight of that keyword should be smaller.

Finally, by adjusting the similarity according to their importance weights, we have the similarity between two videos as follows:

$$\mathbf{C}_{ij} = \begin{cases} 1, & i = j \\ \frac{\sum_{w \in W_i \cap W_j} z_w}{\sum_{w \in W_i \cup W_j} z_w}, & \text{otherwise} \end{cases}.$$

Larger $\mathbf{C}_{ij}$ indicates that content i is more similar to content j.

2.3.2.3 Initial User-Content Matrix

The user-content matrix contains information about how users import and re-share videos in Tencent Weibo. This information is also included in the traces we obtained. To improve the recommendation performance for cold users and cold videos, we can update some missing entries later. Let $\mathbf{B}$ denote the initial user-content matrix as follows:

$$\mathbf{B}_{ij} = \begin{cases} 1, & \text{user } i \text{ has imported/re-shared video } j \\ 0, & \text{otherwise} \end{cases}.$$

In our study, we only use the above "2D" matrices, but they can be extended to have "3D" tensors; e.g., in the user matrix, the social connection between two users can be a vector indicating the different influences of a user to another one, and in the content matrix, more context can be included to measure the similarity (e.g., location). We will discuss the details of the matrix extension in Sect. 2.7.2.

2.3.3 Framework of Our Recommendation

Next, we present the framework of our recommendation, which includes the following key technologies: (1) user-content matrix update based on the social propagation and content similarity and (2) activity-aware user-content space construction.

2.3.3.1 User-Content Matrix Update

As discussed above, the user-content matrix can be very sparse [17]. It is difficult for traditional recombination algorithms to address users who have imported/re-shared no or fewer videos since personalized recommendation is based on users' historical preferences. In our design, we update the user-content matrix by making use of both the social matrix and content matrix to enable recommendation for cold users/videos; that is, we "predict" the items that are likely to be imported/re-shared by a user who has little historical importing/re-sharing information available.

On the one hand, we use the social propagation model to connect users and videos; that is, the videos that are imported/re-shared by a user's friends are likely to be imported/re-shared by the user. On the other hand, we connect videos to users who have imported/re-shared similar videos. Figure 2.3 illustrates the user-content update framework in our design. When updating the user-content matrix $\mathbf{B}'$, besides the initial user-content matrix $\mathbf{B}$, the user-user matrix $\mathbf{A}$ and the content-content matrix $\mathbf{C}$ are also used. In particular, $\mathbf{A}$ and $\mathbf{B}$ are used for the social-propagation-based update, whereas $\mathbf{C}$ and $\mathbf{B}$ are used for the content-similarity-based update. We will discuss the details in Sect. 2.4.

2.3.3.2 Construction of the Joint User-Content Space

Our recommendation is based on constructing a joint user-content space and measuring the relevance between users and content. Figure 2.4 illustrates how the relevance between a user and a video is measured. The joint user-content space is based on combining a user space and a content space. The user space is constructed using

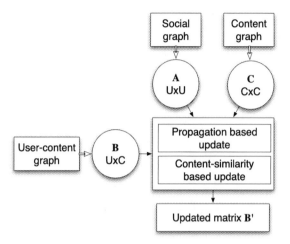

Fig. 2.3 Update of the user-content matrix

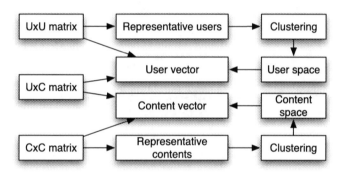

Fig. 2.4 Construction of the user-content space

the user-user matrix, and the content space is constructed using the content-content matrix. A user or a video can be represented by two *description vectors* in both spaces, which have the same dimension. The *relevance* between a user and a video is then measured in both spaces jointly. Finally, videos can be recommended to a user according to their relevance with the user. We will discuss the details in Sect. 2.5.

Before we present the detailed design of the user-content matrix update and the user-content space construction, we list important notation in Table 2.1.

Table 2.1 Notation for understanding user preferences in social video services

Symbol	Definition
A	The user-user matrix
B	The user-content matrix
C	The content-content matrix
$\Omega(\mathbf{M})$	Matrix indicating which entries in **M** are missing
$\mathcal{G}(\mathbf{M})$	Updating gain matrix of **M**
I_{uc}	The update value from social propagation
J_{uc}	The update value from content similarity
E	The candidate set of entries in the user-content matrix for update
L_1	Maximum number of missing entries in the user-content matrix to be updated in each round
L_2	Maximum number of rounds for the update procedure
H	The candidate representative items
R, r	The representative item set and its size
K	The number of clustering groups
$sim(x, y)$	A similarity between x and y
$RE(u, c)$	A relevance index between user u and video c

2.4 User-Content Matrix Update Based on Social Propagation and Content Similarity

We update the initial user-content matrix before performing the relevance-based recommendation.

2.4.1 Selecting the Entries to Update

When choosing the entries in the initial user-content matrix to update, there can be many different principles; e.g., we can target some important users and videos to perform better recommendation for them. In this work, we choose the entries to update as follows: (1) we choose the users/videos with no or few existing entries because these users/videos need more information for recommendation; and (2) we choose the entries that can maximize the "accuracy" when being updated. We will discuss how the two objectives are achieved in turn.

First, we choose the candidate entries that need the information for recommendation. The candidate users/videos to be updated in the user-content matrix are the ones with little information. The update is performed round-by-round: we define the candidate set of entries to update in round T as $\mathbf{E}^{(T)}$. $\mathbf{E}^{(T)}$ is constructed in the following steps: (1) rank users according to the number of videos that they have imported/re-shared recently; (2) select the users with the minimum imported/re-shared videos and choose the videos randomly from a list of representative videos, as discussed in Sect. 2.5; and (3) the selected users/videos then form the candidate set $\mathbf{E}^{(T)}$, $T = 1, 2, \ldots$.

Next, we choose the entries to update according to the accuracy when updating them. To evaluate the accuracy of updating an missing entry, which reflects the level of existing entries when updating it, we define an updating gain as in Eq. (2.1):

$$\mathscr{G}(\mathbf{B}^{(T)})_{ij} = \begin{cases} \begin{cases} 1, & \Omega(\mathbf{B}^{(0)})_{ij} = 1 \\ 0, & \Omega(\mathbf{B}^{(0)})_{ij} = 0 \end{cases} & T = 0 \\ \begin{cases} \mathscr{G}(\mathbf{A})\mathscr{G}(\mathbf{B}^{(T-1)})_{ij} \cdot \mathscr{G}(\mathbf{B}^{(T-1)})\mathscr{G}(\mathbf{C})_{ij}, & \text{Updated in round } T \\ \mathscr{G}(\mathbf{B}^{(T-1)})_{ij}, & \text{otherwise} \end{cases} & T > 0 \end{cases}, \quad (2.1)$$

where $\mathscr{G}(\mathbf{B}^{(T)})_{ij}$ is the updating gain of entry $\mathbf{B}_{ij}$ and $\Omega(\mathbf{B}^{(0)})_{ij} = 1$ indicates $\mathbf{B}_{ij}^{(0)}$ exists in the initial user-content matrix. For matrix $\mathbf{A}$ and $\mathbf{C}$, we have $\mathscr{G}(\mathbf{A})_{ij} = \Omega(\mathbf{A})_{ij}$ and $\mathscr{G}(\mathbf{C})_{ij} = \Omega(\mathbf{C})_{ij}$. The initial updating gain (when $T = 0$) is based on whether the entry exists in the initial user-content matrix; i.e., 1 is assigned to an existing entry, and 0 is assigned to an missing entry. When an entry is updated, the updating gain is evaluated according to how the entry is calculated. In our design, we select the entries in the candidate set $\mathbf{E}^{(T)}$ to maximize the matrix updating gain, by mathematically solving the following problem:

$$\max_{\Gamma} \sum_{(i,j) \in \Gamma} \mathscr{G}(\mathbf{B}^{(T)})_{ij}, \quad (2.2)$$

subject to

$$\Omega(\mathbf{B}^{(T)})_{ij} = 0, (i, j) \in \Gamma,$$

$$\Gamma \subset \mathbf{E}^{(T)},$$

$$|\Gamma| \le L_1,$$

where Γ is the set of entries selected for updating and L_1 is the maximum number of entries to be updated in each round. Next, we discuss how the entries are updated.

2.4.2   Updating the Missing Entries

Next, we will present the user-content matrix update based on the social propagation and content similarity.

First, we discuss the update using social propagation. Figure 2.5a illustrates how social propagation can be used for the recommendation. A video propagates through social connections in a cascading manner [18], where one's interests can influence

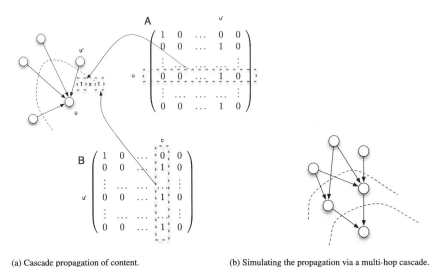

(a) Cascade propagation of content.   (b) Simulating the propagation via a multi-hop cascade.

Fig. 2.5 Update based on social propagation prediction

users. In our design, a row vector $\mathbf{A}_{u,*}$ in the user-user matrix $\mathbf{A}$ indicates the people who are followed by user u, and a column vector $\mathbf{B}_{*,c}$ in the user-content matrix $\mathbf{B}$ indicates the users who have shown interest in video c by importing/re-sharing it. When more people followed by a user have shown interests in a particular video, the user himself can also be influenced. Thus, according to the social propagation, the ability that content c can interest user u is evaluated by

$$I_{uc}^{(T)} = \sum_{k|\Omega(\mathbf{B}^{(T-1)})_{kc}=1} \mathbf{A}_{uk}\mathbf{B}_{kc}^{(T-1)}. \tag{2.3}$$

We update the missing entries in the user-content matrix round by round, based on simulating the propagation of videos through the social connections. As illustrated in Fig. 2.5b, after an entry in the user-content matrix is updated, indicating that the user will potentially import or re-share the video, the user will be able to influence others who follow him. In our algorithm, the parameter L_2 determines the maximum "depth" of the propagation.

Second, we discuss the content similarity based matrix update. Based on a user's historical preference, we can predict what videos the user will be more likely to import/re-share according to the similarity between the videos he has imported/re-shared and other videos. Thus, the ability that a content c can interest user u can be evaluated by

$$J_{uc}^{(T)} = \sum_{k|\Omega(\mathbf{B}^{(T-1)})_{uk}=1} \mathbf{B}_{uk}^{(T-1)}\mathbf{C}_{kc}. \tag{2.4}$$

Algorithm 1 Update of the user-content matrix.

1: **procedure** MATRIX UPDATE($\mathbf{A}$, $\mathbf{B}^{(0)} = \mathbf{B}$, $\mathbf{C}$)
2:    $t \leftarrow 0$
3:    **while** $t < L_2$ **do**
4:       According to Eq. (2.1), calculate the updating gains for entries in $\mathbf{E}^{(t)}$
5:       Rank the entries in $\mathbf{E}^{(t)}$ in their updating gains' descending order
6:       **for** the top L_1 entries in the ranked entry list **do**
7:          Update the selected L_1 entries using Eq. (2.5)
8:       **end for**
9:       $t \leftarrow t + 1$
10:   **end while**
11: **end procedure**

Finally, a missing entry is updated according to the combination of $I_{uc}^{(T)}$ and $J_{uc}^{(T)}$:

$$\mathbf{B}_{uc}^{(T)} = \begin{cases} 1, I_{uc}^{(T)} \cdot J_{uc}^{(T)} > \eta \\ 0, otherwise \end{cases}, \tag{2.5}$$

where η is the threshold to determine the updating result. In each update round, η is dynamically adjusted such that at least half of the candidate entries are updated to 1. The algorithm for the user-content matrix update is given in Algorithm 1.

2.5 User-Content Space Construction and the Recommendation

We construct the user-content space after the user-content matrix has been updated. In our design, we describe each user and each video by a vector in the user-content space such that the *relevance* of a user and a video can be measured for the recommendation.

2.5.1 Construction of the Joint User-Content Space

We first construct the user space and content space separately such that a user and a video can be mapped into either of the spaces. Then, we combine the vectors in both spaces to measure the relevance between a user and a video according to the dot product of their vectors in the joint user-content space to perform the recommendation.

Algorithm 2 Selection of representative items.

1: **procedure** REPRESENTATIVE ITEM SELECT(**H**)
2:     Select r items randomly from **H** to form a initial **R**
3:     Find item $m \in \mathbf{R}$ that has the largest similarity cost $cost(m, \mathbf{R}, \mathbf{H})$
4:     Replace item m with item n selected from $\mathbf{H} - \mathbf{R}$, which has the smallest similarity cost
5:     Repeat 2–4 until the similarity cost change is smaller than threshold TH_{select}
6: **end procedure**

2.5.1.1 A General Algorithm for User/Content Space Construction

Since the user space and content space are constructed using similar procedures, we present the general algorithm that is employed in both user space and content space construction.

Choose r representative items from a candidate set. Let $sim(x, y)$ denote the similarity between item x and item y (an item can be a user or a video). A larger $sim(x, y)$ indicates that x is more similar to y. In our design, we choose r representative items from the candidate set by solving the following problem:

$$\min_{\mathbf{R}} \sum_{x \neq y, x, y \in \mathbf{R}} sim(x, y), \tag{2.6}$$

subject to

$$\mathbf{R} \subset \mathbf{H},$$

$$|\mathbf{R}| = r,$$

where **R** is the set of the selected representative items and **H** is the whole candidate set. The rationale of the optimization in Eq. (2.6) is that we select representative items that are sufficiently "different" from each other to maximize their ability to describe the diversity of other items. The problem can be solved by using the heuristic algorithm presented in Algorithm 2. First, it randomly chooses r items from the candidate set and then replaces the items to obtain a better set iteratively by reducing a similarity cost, which is defined as follows:

$$cost(m, \mathbf{R}, \mathbf{H}) = \sum_{x \neq m, x \in \mathbf{R}} sim(m, x). \tag{2.7}$$

Below, we will discuss the candidate items and the number of representative items for the user space and content space.

Cluster the r representative items into K groups. We define *description index* for a group of several representative items, which is a similar concept used in the clustering algorithms, e.g., K-Means and K-Medoids [35], to evaluate the similarity between items within a group. A larger description index indicates that items are more closely clustered inside the group. We maximize the description index within

---

Algorithm 3 Clustering of the representative items.

1: **procedure** REPRESENTATIVE ITEM CLUSTER(**R**)
2:     Randomly select K items $\{e_1, e_2, \ldots, e_K\}$ from **R** as the initial medoids
3:     **for** $\forall x \, in \, \mathbf{R} - \{e_1, e_2, \ldots, e_K\}$ **do**
4:         Assign x to a group whose medoid is the most similar to x
5:     **end for**
6:     For each group, replace the medoid with an item in the same group such that the *clustering gain* can be maximized
7:     Repeat 2–6 until the clustering gain change is smaller than threshold $TH_{cluster}$
8: **end procedure**

---

the same group as follows:

$$\max_{G} \sum_{g \in G} \sum_{x \in g} ra(x, g), \tag{2.8}$$

subject to

$$|G| = K,$$

$$g_i \cap g_j = \Phi, g_i, g_j \in G, i \neq j,$$

$$\cup_i g_i = \mathbf{R},$$

where G is the set of groups we choose for the space construction, g is a group in G, and $ra(x, g)$ defines a representative index of item x in group g. The representative index is defined as

$$ra(x, g) = \sum_{y \neq x, y \in g} sim(x, y)/|g|. \tag{2.9}$$

We use a K-Medoids-like algorithm to solve the above optimization, as illustrated in Algorithm 3. First, K initial medoids are randomly selected from the representative set **R**; then, we change the medoids to other items to improve the clustering gain, which is defined as follows:

$$gain(x, x_0) = \sum_{y \neq x, y \in g} sim(x, y) - \sum_{y \neq x_0, y \in g} sim(x_0, y), \tag{2.10}$$

where x_0 is the original medoid of a group. By improving the clustering gain iteratively, we are able to increase the description index of the groups.

Map any user/video to a K-dimension vector. In the user space, a user u will be described as a vector p_u, and a video c will be described as a vector $\bar{p}_c$, whereas in the content space, a user u will be described as a vector q_u, and a video c will be described as a vector $\bar{q}_c$. We define a relevance index between u and c as follows:

$$RE(u, c, m) = \alpha p_u \cdot \bar{p}_c + (1 - \alpha) q_u \cdot \bar{q}_c, \tag{2.11}$$

where α is a dynamical weight to combine the relevance values in both the user space and content space. A large α indicates that the user will be more likely to refer to the user space for the recommendation, whereas small α indicates that he is more likely to refer to the content space for the recommendation. We will further evaluate and discuss the impact of this parameter in Sect. 2.6.

Next, we will discuss in particular how the user space and content space are constructed.

2.5.1.2 Construction of the User Space

Based on the user-user matrix generated from the Weibo traces, we present how the user space is constructed using the general algorithms.

Select the representative users. In Weibo, some users are so famous that they have millions of followers; these users are distributed in different categories, such as IT and business. They can be used as the representative users. Figure 2.6 illustrates the number of followers of each user in the 5,000 top-followed users (who have the largest numbers of followers in Tencent Weibo), ranked according to the numbers of their followers. We observe that the number of followers of the top-followed users is much greater than that of the average user.

To avoid the impact of the most popular users who can be easily followed by anyone, we skip the first 1,000 top-followed users. Figure 2.7 illustrates the number of people covered by the top 1,000–4,0000 followed users, i.e., the users who have followed at least one of the top-followed users. We observe the 3,000 top-followed users can cover approximately 20 million users in the system, which is approximately the number of all users in Tencent Weibo. Thus, we choose the 1,000–4,000 top-followed users as the representative users.

In our design, the similarity $sim(u, v)$ between two users is calculated as the fraction of their common followers as follows:

Fig. 2.6 Number of followers of the top-followed users

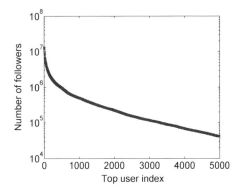

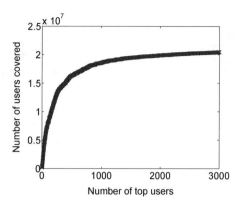

Fig. 2.7 The number of covered users vs. the number of top-followed users

$$sim(u, v) = \frac{|fans(u) \cap fans(v)|}{|fans(u) \cup fans(v)|}, \tag{2.12}$$

where $fans(u)$ is the set of users who follow u in Weibo. The rationale is as follows. (1) *Weak social relations.* Compared with the strong social connections (friends) in social network systems like Facebook, the following relation in a microblogging system can be very weak; i.e., users can follow anyone who interests them. (2) *Interest based on following connections between ordinary users and top-followed users.* Since users can follow users all according to their own interests, the fraction of common followers of two top-followed users can be used to represent their similarity. Facebook has also confirmed that weak relationships can represent users' interests and are important sources of information about users [12].

Cluster the representative users. We need to solve the optimization given in Eq. (2.8) to obtain the groups used to construct the user space. We have already defined the similarity between users, and we are able to directly use Algorithm 3 to cluster the top-followed users. In our experiments, we choose K_U to be approximately 20.

Construct user vector and content vector in the user space. The user vector and content vector are constructed as follows.

- User vector in user space (p_u). Let f_{iu}^1 denote the number of representative users in group i that user u follows. The user vector is the normalization of vector $\{f_{1u}^1, f_{2u}^1, \ldots, f_{K_U u}^1\}$, i.e., entry p_{ui} in p_u is defined as $p_{ui} = \frac{f_{iu}^1}{\sum_k f_{ku}^1}$. The rationale is that when user u follows more representative users in a group, the corresponding entry in the user vector is larger to emphasize his interest in that particular group.
- Content vector in user space ($\bar{p}_c$). We use the updated user-content matrix to construct the content vector p_c. Let f_{ic}^2 denote the aggregate strength of users who have imported/re-shared video c, $f_{ic}^2 = \sum_{k \in U_c} p_{kc}$, where U_c is the set of users who have imported or re-shared video c. The content vector is then defined as the normalization of vector $\{f_{1c}^2, f_{2c}^2, \ldots, f_{K_U c}^2\}$; i.e., entry $\bar{p}_{ci}$ in $\bar{p}_c$ is defined as

Fig. 2.8 Fraction of users covered by the top-imported/re-shared videos

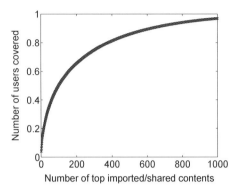

$\bar{p}_{ci} = \frac{f_{ic}^2}{\sum_k f_{kc}^2}$. The rationale is that a large entry in $\bar{p}_c$ indicates that more users from the corresponding group likes that video.

2.5.1.3 Construction of the Content Space

Similarly, we present how we construct the content space using the general algorithm.

Select the representative videos. We choose the representative contents from the top-imported/re-shared videos, which are the most popular ones which have the largest number of viewers. Figure 2.8 illustrates the fraction of users covered by the top-imported/re-shared contents in Tencent Weibo; i.e., the users have imported/re-shared at least one video in the top-imported/re-shared videos. In our design, we use $r_C = 400$ candidate top-imported/re-shared videos, which can cover almost 80% of all the users. The content similarity is defined in Sect. 2.3.2, i.e., $sim(x, y) = \mathbf{C}_{xy}$. We choose the representative content using Algorithm 2.

Cluster the representative videos. We have selected the top-imported/re-shared videos that are the most popular ones in the system. To maximize the description index of the selected videos, we need to cluster these top-imported/re-shared videos into multiple groups. We use Algorithm 3 to cluster the representative videos to groups. In our experiments, the performance can be optimized when the number K_C of clusters is approximately 8.

Construct content vector and user vector in the content space. The content vector and user vector are constructed as follows.

- Content vector in content space ($\bar{q}_c$). Let f_{ic}^3 denote the aggregate similarity of video c with all items in group i, i.e., $f_{ic}^3 = \sum_{k \in g_i} \mathbf{C}_{kc}$. The content vector then is defined as the normalization of vector $\{f_{1c}^3, f_{2c}^3, \ldots, f_{K_Cc}^3\}$, i.e., entry $\bar{q}_{ci}$ in $\bar{q}_c$ is defined as $\bar{q}_{ci} = \frac{f_{ic}^3}{\sum_k f_{kc}^3}$. The rationale is that a larger entry in $\bar{q}_c$ indicates that video c is more similar to that group.
- User vector in content space (q_u). Let f_{ui}^4 denote the aggregate strength of content that has been imported/re-shared by user u, $f_{ui}^4 = \sum_{k \in V_u} \bar{q}_{ck}$, where V_u is the set of

videos that are imported or re-shared by u. The user vector q_u is the normalization of vector $\{f_{u1}^4, f_{u2}^4, \ldots, f_{uK_C}^4\}$, i.e., entry q_{ui} in q_u is defined as $q_{ui} = \frac{f_{ui}^4}{\sum_k f_{uk}^4}$. The rationale is that if user u has imported/re-shared more videos similar to a group, the corresponding entry in the user vector should be larger to reflect his interest in that group.

2.5.2 Recommendation Based on the User-Content Space

After the user space and content space have been constructed, the relevance between a user and a video can be measured according to Eq. (2.11). The recommendation is provided to a user as a list of the videos that have the largest relevance index with the user. In our design, we provide the importing list and re-sharing list as follows.

- *Importing list.* The importing list contains videos that are likely to be imported by users to the microblogging system. Since a user is able to view all videos on external video sharing sites such as Youku, the candidate video pool contains all of the recently popular videos on Youku, and the importing list generated by our algorithm is the ones with the largest relevance index with the user. When importing a video, a user considers more about the video itself; thus, a smaller α will be used when performing the importing recommendation.
- *Re-sharing list.* The re-sharing list contains videos that are the most likely to be re-shared by a user further to his followers. Since the videos that the user can re-share are the ones imported or re-shared from people he follows. Thus, the candidate video pool for the re-sharing recommendation is the list of videos that can "reach" them, i.e., the ones that have been re-shared by people they follow. When re-sharing a video, a user considers not only the video but also the friends who imports/re-shares the video. Thus, a larger α will be used when performing the re-sharing recommendation.

2.6 Experimental Results

In this section, we conduct experiments using real traces from Tencent Weibo and Youku to verify our algorithm and evaluate its performance.

2.6.1 Experiment Setup

We evaluate the performance of our joint social-content recommendation for both video importing and video re-sharing. We use traces from Tencent Weibo and Youku to run the experiments. We randomly chose 2200 videos from Youku, which were selected from the 5 most popular categories on Youku. The videos were published between March 19 and June 20, 2011, and were the most popular ones on Youku's front pages on June 20, 2011. Approximately 600,000 users have imported or re-shared these videos. In particular, the traces contain the following information. (1) The user-user matrix. The traces record the social connections, i.e., which users are followed by which users. (2) The content-content matrix. The traces record the original URLs of the videos, which can be used to crawl their text tags, which are used to generate the matrix as presented in Sect. 2.3.2.2. (3) The initial user-content matrix. The microblog traces also record whether a video is imported or re-shared, and we generate the initial user-content matrix by setting the entry to 1 if the user has imported or re-shared the video.

In our experiments, we use the recommendation accuracy as the key performance metric, which is the fraction of videos that are correctly suggested by the recommender system over all the videos imported/re-shared by users [4]. After we provide a recommendation list to users, by comparing it with their true importing or re-sharing records, we can yield the recommendation accuracy. In the following experiments, we divide the user-content matrix into two parts: 60% of the records will be used as the input of the initial user-content matrix, and the rest will be used as the ground truth to evaluate the design.

2.6.2 Algorithm Verification

In Fig. 2.9, we first evaluate the impact of the user space and content space. The two curves in this figure illustrate the recommendation accuracy versus α for importing recommendation and re-sharing recommendation, respectively. We observe that for both recommendation, too large or too small α leads to low recommendation accuracy. The reason is that when recommending importing and re-sharing videos to users, the relevance between users and videos in both user space (where users and videos are represented by representative user groups) and content space (where users and videos are represented by representative content groups) can assist the recommendation, and the recommendation based on a combination of the relevance in both spaces achieves the best performance. From this figure, we observe that the importing recommendation relies more on the content space, i.e., a relatively small α (0.3) achieves the best accuracy, whereas the re-sharing recommendation relies more on the user space, i.e., a relatively large α (0.7) achieves the best performance. The reason is that the importing activity is performed more according to users' interests in videos, whereas re-sharing is usually performed more according to the people that a user follows. The results verify the effectiveness of our joint social-content approach for both importing and re-sharing recommendations. In other experiments, we use $\alpha = 0.3$ and $\alpha = 0.7$ for importing recommendations and re-sharing recommendations, respectively. $\alpha = 0$ will be referred to as using the content space only, and $\alpha = 1$ will be referred to as using the user space only.

Fig. 2.9 Recommendation
accuracy vs. α

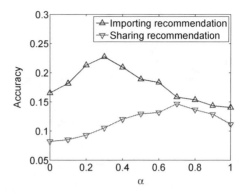

Since personalized recommendation relies on users' historical preferences, we evaluate the performance by varying the number of users' historical importing and re-sharing records. Users with more importing/re-sharing records are referred to as more active users. The user-content matrix update based on social propagation and content similarity is expected to improve the recommendation for cold users/contents. In our experiments, we evaluate the recommendation for users with fewer re-sharing/importing records in the system. Specifically, we randomly choose 100, 000 users from the most inactive users for the evaluation. First, we evaluate the impact of L_1, which determines the number of missing entries to update in each round. Figure 2.10 illustrates the recommendation accuracy versus the number of missing entries updated in each round. In Fig. 2.10a, we observe that for the importing recommendation, when more missing entries are updated, higher accuracy can be achieved, and when the number is too large, the increase rate is smaller. In Fig. 2.10b, similar results are observed for the re-sharing recommendation, but with a smaller increase rate. Second, we evaluate the impact of the number of rounds used for the user-content matrix update. The number of rounds used in updating the missing entries determines the depth of the propagation simulation. Figure 2.11a, b illustrate the recommendation accuracy versus the number of updating rounds used in the update. We observe that the best accuracy can be achieved when the number of updating rounds is between 2 and 3 for both importing and re-sharing recommendation, indicating that in the update, a moderate propagation depth should be used.

2.6.3 Performance Evaluation

We first evaluate the performance of our own design under different combinations of the user space and content space. Figure 2.12a, b illustrate the recommendation accuracy versus the number of top-active users used in the evaluation. From the two figures we can see that when more inactive users are evaluated, the accuracy is

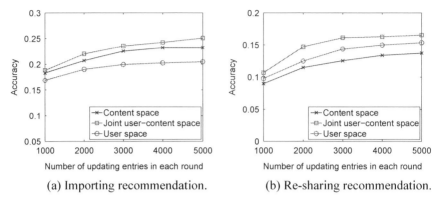

(a) Importing recommendation.   (b) Re-sharing recommendation.

Fig. 2.10 Accuracy vs. the number of entries filled (l_1) in the user-content update

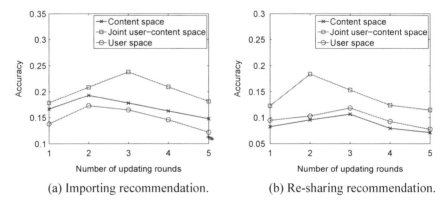

(a) Importing recommendation.   (b) Re-sharing recommendation.

Fig. 2.11 Accuracy vs. the updating rounds (L_2) in the user-content update

decreased. Meanwhile, we observe that comparing with using only the user space ($\alpha = 1$) or only the content space ($\alpha = 0$), the user-content space achieves better performance. Similarly, we also observe that the content space achieves better performance than the user space in importing recommendation, whereas the user space achieves better performance than the content space in re-sharing recommendation.

We also compare our approach with the following algorithms: the content-based filtering approach [25] and the collaborative filtering approach [26]. Although the approaches are not directly designed to perform recommendations in our scenario, i.e., the importing recommendation and re-sharing recommendation for user-generated videos in an online social network, we implement them as follows. (1) Content-based filtering approach. For each user, the videos he has imported/re-shared are used to find the new ones that may interest him. Videos that are the most similar to the ones he has imported/re-shared before are recommended (according to the content-content matrix). The size of the recommendation list is the same as that used in our approach. (2) Collaborative filtering approach. In the collaborative filtering

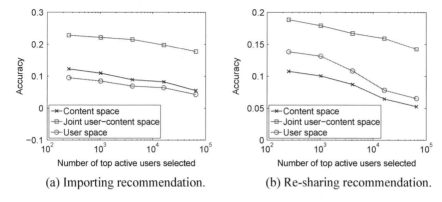

(a) Importing recommendation.   (b) Re-sharing recommendation.

Fig. 2.12 Accuracy vs. the number of top-active users under different combinations of user space and content space

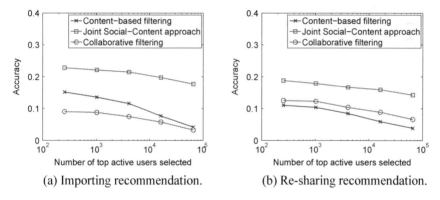

(a) Importing recommendation.   (b) Re-sharing recommendation.

Fig. 2.13 Comparison of the joint social-content recommendation with the content-based filtering and collaborative filtering approaches

approach, "similar" users are discovered according to the videos they have imported or re-shared, i.e., two users are more similar to each other if they have imported or re-shared more common videos before. The recommendation list for a user consists of the videos that are imported/re-shared by users who are the most similar to him.

Figure 2.13 illustrates the recommendation accuracy of different recommendation algorithms in terms of the number of top-active users used in the evaluation. In general, we observe that for both importing and re-sharing recommendations, our approach achieves significantly higher recommendation accuracy, especially when more users with little importing/re-sharing history are involved in the evaluation. We also observe that content-based filtering works better in the importing recommendation, whereas collaborative filtering works slightly better in the re-sharing recommendation.

2.7 Discussion

To further explore the potential of the joint social and content recommendation in a real large-scale online social network service, in this section, we discuss the efficiency of our recommendation algorithms and how they can be extended to satisfy more complicated social connections and video properties.

2.7.1 Efficiency of the Recommendation Algorithms

First, we discuss the efficiency of the user-content matrix update. The update algorithm is able to adapt to the Internet-scale social media recommendation thanks to the unique characteristics of the online social network: (1) *The number of a user's social connections is limited*. Dunbar's number [2] is suggested as a theoretical cognitive limit to the number (150) of people with whom one can maintain stable social relations. In our measurement of Tencent Weibo, we observe that the average number of people one follows is less than 100. When performing the social-propagation-based update, the limited number of social connections of a user can largely reduce the amount of computation. (2) *The number of video candidates for recommendation is limited*. In the online social network, users are more likely to exchange and consume recent content. In our measurement study of Tencent Weibo, we observe that the majority of the videos that users import and re-share are published in the past 24 h [33]. Thus, in our recommendation, the size of the candidate videos can be quite limited. (3) *The number of entries to update is limited*. In our algorithm, the number of entries in the user-content matrix to be updated can be dynamically adjusted according to the load of the recommendation system and the number of active users; e.g., the update will be performed when a user is actively requesting the recommendation list and the system is able to handle the load. Otherwise, the system will perform the recommendation with a lower quality when the update is not performed for some users.

Second, we discuss the efficiency of the space construction. (1) To maintain the set of the representative users or videos, a heap data structure can be utilized such that changes to the representative users only require $\log(r)$ comparisons and switches. (2) In our clustering algorithm, we use the threshold $TH_{cluster}$ to limit the rounds. (3) When calculating a user's vectors, only numbers, rather than detailed content, are used, i.e., the number of a user's idols and the number of videos he has viewed are utilized (the number of the videos one has viewed is limited since only the recent viewing history is referred to). Similarly, the space construction can scale for the large recommendation.

---

[2]http://en.wikipedia.org/wiki/Dunbar's_number.

2.7.2 Extension of the Matrix

In this study, for each matrix, an entry is a numerical value to indicate the social connection, social activity and content similarity; however, when performing recommendations, more complicated information can be explored, e.g., the location and gender of a user or the category and duration of a video. To incorporate such information into our recommendation, we can extend the 2D matrices to 3D matrices. Let Z denote the number of these context items we can use; each entry in the three matrices will be replaced by a Z-dimensional vector. In the user-user matrix, $\mathbf{a_{ij}} = \{e_1, e_2, \ldots, e_Z\}$ indicates the different aspects of how user j can affect user i; in the user-content matrix, $\mathbf{b_{ij}} = \{e'_1, e'_2, \ldots, e'_Z\}$ indicates the different aspects of how user i likes video j; and in the content-content matrix, $\mathbf{c_{ij}} = \{e''_1, e''_2, \ldots, e''_Z\}$ indicates the different aspects of how content i is similar to j. In the user-content matrix update and the relevance space construction, the original operations of the matrix entries will be replaced by the operations of the vectors, e.g., $\sum_k \mathbf{a_{ik}}^\mathsf{T} \cdot \mathbf{b_{kj}} \cdot \sum_k \mathbf{b_{ik}}^\mathsf{T} \cdot \mathbf{c_{kj}}$ will be the value to compare with the threshold η in the user-content matrix update. Since we lack such extensive information from our current traces from Tencent Weibo and Youku, we would like to explore the potential of 3D tensors in future work.

References

1. M. Arlitt, B. Krishnamurthy, P. Gill, A few chirps about twitter, in *ACM Workshop on Online Social Networks (WOSN)* (2008)
2. S. Baluja et al., Video suggestion and discovery for youtube: taking random walks through the view graph, in *ACM International Conference on World Wide Web (WWW)* (2008)
3. J. Basilico, T. Hofmann, Unifying collaborative and content-based filtering, in *ACM International Conference on Machine Learning* (2004)
4. C. Basu, H. Hirsh, W. Cohen, et al., Recommendation as classification: using social and content-based information in recommendation, in *Proceedings of the National Conference on Artificial Intelligence* (Wiley, 1998), pp. 714–720
5. F. Benevenuto et al., Characterizing user behavior in online social Networks, in *ACM Internet Measurement Conference (IMC)* (2009)
6. M. Cha et al., I tube, you tube, everybody tubes: analyzing the world's largest user generated content video system, in *ACM SIGCOMM* (2007), pp. 1–14
7. T. Coppens, L. Trappeniers, M. Godon, AmigoTV: towards a social TV experience, in *European Conference on Interactive Television "Enhancing the Experience"* (2004)
8. J. Davidson et al., The youtube video recommendation system, in *ACM Recommender Systems* (2010)
9. S. Debnath, N. Ganguly, P. Mitra, Feature weighting in content based recommendation system using social network analysis, in *ACM International Conference on World Wide Web (WWW)* (2008)
10. P.S. Dodds, D.J. Watts, A generalized model of social and biological contagion. J. Theor. Biol. **232**(4), 587–604 (2005)
11. P. Domingos, M. Richardson, Mining the network value of customers, in *ACM SIGKDD Conference on Knowledge Discovery and Data Mining (KDD)* (2001)
12. N.B. Ellison, C. Steinfield, C. Lampe, The benefits of Facebook "Friends:" social capital and college students' use of online social network sites. J. Comput.-Med. Commun. **12.4**, 1143–1168 (2007)

13. J. Hartline, V. Mirrokni, M. Sundararajan, Optimal marketing strategies over social networks, in *ACM International Conference on World Wide Web (WWW)* (2008)
14. J.L. Herlocker, J.A. Konstan, J. Riedl, Explaining collaborative filtering recommendations, in *ACM Conference on Computer Supported Cooperative Work* (2000), pp. 241–250
15. J.L. Herlocker et al., Evaluating collaborative filtering recommender systems. ACM Trans. Inf. Syst. (TOIS) **22**(1), 5–53 (2004)
16. S. Isaacman et al., Distributed rating prediction in user generated content streams, in *ACM Recommender Systems* (2011)
17. C.R. Johnson, Matrix completion problems: a survey, in *Matrix Theory and Applications*, vol. 40 (Amer Mathematical Society, 1990), pp. 171–198
18. D. Kempe, J. Kleinberg, Tardos, Maximizing the spread of influence through a social network, in *ACM SIGKDD Conference on Knowledge Discovery and Data Mining (KDD)* (2003)
19. Y. Koren, The bellkor solution to the netflix grand prize, in *Netflix Prize Documentation* (2009)
20. H. Kwak et al., What Is Twitter, a social network or a news media?, in *ACM International Conference on World Wide Web (WWW)* (2010)
21. G. Linden, B. Smith, J. York, Amazon. com recommendations: itemto-item collaborative filtering, in *Internet Computing, IEEE 7.1* (2003), pp. 76–80
22. P. Melville, R.J. Mooney, R. Nagarajan, Content-boosted collaborative filtering for improved recommendations, in *The National Conference on Artificial Intelligence* (2002)
23. A. Mislove et al., Measurement and analysis of online social networks, in *ACM Internet Measurement Conference (IMC)* (2007)
24. L. Oehlberg, N. Ducheneaut, J.D. Thornton, R.J. Moore, E. Nickell, Social TV: designing for distributed, sociable television viewing, in *EuroITV* (2006)
25. M. Pazzani, D. Billsus, Content-based recommendation systems, in *The Adaptive Webed*, ed. by P. Brusilovsky, A. Kobsa, W. Nejdl (Springer-Verlag, 2007), pp. 325–341
26. B. Sarwar et al., Item-based collaborative filtering recommendation algorithms, *ACM International Conference on World Wide Web (WWW)* (ACM, 2001), pp. 285–295
27. J. Schafer et al., Collaborative filtering recommender systems, in *The Adaptive Web* (2007), pp. 291–324
28. R. Schatz et al., Mobile TV becomes social-integrating content with communications, in *IEEE International Conference on Information Technology Interfaces* (2007)
29. "Tencent Weibo". http://t.qq.com/
30. F.E. Walter, S. Battiston, F. Schweitzer, A model of a trust-based recommendation system on a social network. Auton. Agents Multi-Agent Syst. **16**(1), 57–74 (2008)
31. X. Wang et al., Group recommendation using external followee for social TV, in *IEEE International Conference on Multimedia and Expo (ICME)* (2012)
32. Z. Wang et al., Prefetching strategy in peer-assisted social video streaming, in *International Conference on Multimedia (Multimedia)* (2011)
33. Z. Wang et al., Propagation-based social-aware replication for social video contents, in *ACM International Conference on Multimedia (Multimedia)* (2012)
34. M.M.L.Wasko, S. Faraj, Why should i share? examining social capital and knowledge contribution in electronic networks of practice, in *Mis Quarterly* (2005), pp. 35–57
35. R. Xu, D. Wunsch et al., Survey of clustering algorithms. IEEE Trans. Neural Netw. **16**(3), 645–678 (2005)
36. YouTube. http://www.youtube.com/yt/press/statistics.html
37. R. Zhou, S. Khemmarat, L. Gao, The impact of YouTube recommendation system on video views, in *ACM Internet Measurement Conference (IMC)* (2010)

Chapter 3
Enhancing Multimedia Network Resource Allocation Using Social Prediction

Abstract Network resource allocation is the foundation for content delivery. In an online social network, prediction of social behaviors provides an indicator for resource allocation. This chapter presents strategies to enhance the performance of network resource allocation based on the prediction of social behaviors.

Keywords Online content popularity · social propagation · popularity prediction

3.1 Introduction

Recent years have witnessed the blossom of microblogging services in the Internet, e.g., Twitter, Google+, Plurk. In a microblogging system, users can create and maintain social connections among each other, in addition to subscribe to contents shared by others from external content sharing system, as followers [11]. Among the variety of contents to exchange, links to videos on video sharing sites are a popular type—users from microblogging exchanges constitute a large portion of viewers in YouTube-like video sharing sites [12]. Popularity patterns of such *socialized* videos have greatly changed as follows: (1) video popularity is highly affected by online social networks and (2) popularity has become more instantaneous [5]. These changes make traditional popularity-based approaches for video service deployment suboptimal, if not completely ineffective [24].[1]

Since a microblogging system is closely connected to many content sharing sites, it ideally samples valuable information about how users produce and share content from those sites. Video propagation models in a microblogging system can be exploited for a better prediction of video popularity patterns to improve the service quality of a video sharing system. In this chapter, we advocate exploiting the sampling and prediction capabilities of a microblogging system to provide better Internet video services.

In a typical video sharing site today, large volumes of videos are uploaded by users, with viewers from all over the world. In 2013, more than 100 h worth of videos were

---

[1] ©[2015] IEEE. Reprinted, with permission, from IEEE Transactions on Parallel and Distributed Systems.

© The Author(s) 2018   33
Z. Wang et al., *Online Social Media Content Delivery*,
SpringerBriefs in Computer Science, https://doi.org/10.1007/978-981-10-2774-1_3

uploaded every minute on YouTube, serving up to 1 billion unique viewers every month. A common practice to provide these video services is to replicate videos in servers at different geographic locations [1], but it is impractical to replicate all the videos in every location. An effective and adaptive replication strategy to serve the dynamic demand for different videos in different geographic regions is needed.

In this chapter, we propose exploiting video sharing patterns from a microblogging system for this purpose. The potential benefits are two-fold: (1) a video sharing site typically has no information about how video views propagate among its users, and a view propagation model could enable more effective view prediction; and (2) the exchanges of video links in a microblogging system typically happen earlier than the actually video views on a video sharing site, and the time lag between both events can allow more timely and proactive deployment of videos. Based on our preliminary findings of the connection between the popularity of a video and how the video is shared via a microblogging system [23], in this chapter, we focus on employing video microblog propagation patterns to improve the deployment of video services. Our contributions can be summarized as follows.

- In Sect. 3.3, we explore connections between microblogging exchanges of video links and popularity of videos, based on extensive traces collected from Tencent Weibo (hereafter, Weibo, a Twitter-like Chinese microblogging system) and Youku (an Internet video sharing site with immense popularity in China). We identify important characteristics of Weibo, which influence video access patterns on Youku: (1) the number of users that have *imported* a video to Weibo, (2) the number of users that *re-share* links to the video to their followers, (3) the number of followers that the video link share can reach, and (4) the *geographic distribution* of Weibo users.
- In Sect. 3.4, we exploit these influential factors in the design of a neural network-based learning framework for predicting the number of potential viewers of different videos and the geographic distribution of viewers. The accuracy of our prediction models is verified by trace-driven cross-validation experiments, where we compare the results of our models to those of the classical approach of linear regression-based forecasting.
- In Sect. 3.5, we further design a proactive video deployment algorithm based on the prediction frameworks. The algorithm can significantly improve the video download performance of users, according to our trace-driven experiments.

3.2 Related Work

Many architectures have been proposed to implement a large-scale video service, which distributes videos to users across the Internet as follows. (1) *Server-based strategies*, e.g., content distribution networks (CDNs) [17], which power today's dominating HTTP streaming. (2) *Client-based strategies*, e.g., peer-to-peer content distribution is widely used in live video distribution and on-demand video distribution [14]. (3) *Hybrid strategies*, e.g., a hybrid CDN and P2P distribution framework [26]. Traditional video distributions generally work in a passive manner in that video replication and caching are scheduled according to the video access patterns perceived by the servers or peers, e.g., using linear regression approach to infer the future popularity of a video [15].

Video services in the Web 2.0 era focus more on the "social effects", including user experience, user participation and interaction with rich media. The impact of such social effects is fundamental because of not only the huge amount of videos generated by users but also the change in the video popularity distribution [6]. Li et al. [13] have studied the video sharing in online social networks and observed the skewed popularity distribution of content and the power-law activity of users. Traditional video distribution strategies designed without the consideration of such social influence achieve sub-optimal performance in distributing videos in the context of online social network. Saxena et al. [20] have revealed that at some locations, the average service delay of YouTube can be as large as 6.5 s, due to inefficient replication and distribution strategies [1], e.g., slow reactions to popularity changes.

Only by carefully considering social network information can video sharing systems effectively distribute social/socialized video content. Krishnamurthy et al. [3] have investigated an online microblogging system, Twitter, and identified distinct classes of Twitter users and their behaviors as well as the geographic growth patterns of the social network.

With increasing popularity, microblogging systems resemble real society. The interests, beliefs, and behavior of users in a microblogging system are representative of those in the real world [19]. To exploit the similarities, Ritterman et al. [18] advocated to forecast a swine flu pandemic based on a belief change model summarized from Twitter. In context of content popularity prediction based on a microblogging system, different models have been used for prediction in a variety of scenarios, including various linear regression models [16] and machine learning models [25]. Yang et al. [27] investigate the prediction of information diffusion in Twitter in terms of the speed, scale, and range. Szabo et al. [22] study how to predict the popularity of content on Digg and YouTube, using their own historical popularities. To the best of our knowledge, we are not aware of any existing study exploiting characteristics of a microblogging system to predict video access in another *external* video sharing system.

3.3 Measurements and Analysis

3.3.1 Collection of Traces

We have obtained traces from Youku and Weibo as follows.

Youku. In our study, we collected 2,291 representative videos from 5 popular categories on Youku: "Music", "News", "Entertainment", "Baby" and "Original". As

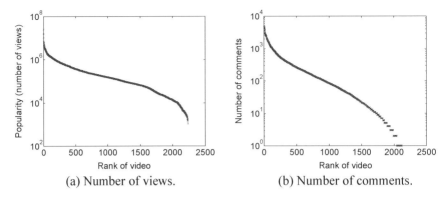

Fig. 3.1 Popularity of the sampled videos

video sharing systems usually do not share detailed video popularity information, we crawled the view numbers of the videos periodically to study their popularity change over time. The crawling was performed from June 20 to June 30, 2011, on an hourly basis to avoid being blocked from frequent crawling. Each trace log indicates the cumulative number of views of each video since when the video was published until when the log was recorded, based on which we can calculate the average number of views of a video in each hour.

These 2, 291 videos cover a large range of popularity in terms of the number of views and comments. As illustrated in Fig. 3.1a, each sample represents the total number of views of a video since its publication until the end of the ten days versus the rank of the video. In Fig. 3.1b, each sample represents the total number of comments posted by users (Youku allows users to post comments to videos) starting from its publication to the end of the ten days versus the rank of the video. We observe that our dataset contains representative videos in a sense that they cover a large range of popularity.

Tencent Weibo. We obtained Weibo traces from the technical team of Tencent; these traces contain valuable runtime data regarding the system for all of June 2011. Each entry in the traces corresponds to one microblog published, including the ID, name, IP address of the publisher, time stamp when the microblog was posted, IDs of the parent and root microbloggers if it is a re-post, and content of the microblog. We parsed the traces and obtained 4,468,398 microblogs related to the videos above, i.e., the microblogs that either contain the links to the videos or are re-shares of the microblogs that contain the links. In our study, we also used the social relationships between users involved in these microblogs.

Before starting our measurement study, we first present the important notation used in this chapter in Table 3.1.

Table 3.1 Notation in network resource allocation

Symbol	Definition
$R_v^T(i)$	The number of root users of video v in the ith time slot in the time window before T
$S_v^T(i)$	The number of re-share users of video v in the ith time slot in the time window before T
$I_v^T(i)$	The number of influenced users of video v in the ith time slot in the time window before T
$G_{v,r}^T$	The fraction of microblogs of video v posted by users in region r in time slot T
X_v^T	The input features for the prediction of the number of views of video v in time slot T
$\bar{V}_v^T$	The level of views of video v in time slot T
Y_v^T	The input features for the prediction of the geographic distribution of views of video v in time slot T
$\alpha(i)$	The weight to adjust the input features in the ith time slot for the prediction of view number
$\beta(i)$	The weight to adjust the input features in the ith time slot for the prediction of view geographic distribution
M	The number of previous days when features are collected for prediction
$\mathscr{R}$	The set of geographic regions
$\mathscr{V}$	The set of videos
$V_{v,r}^T$	The number of concurrent requests for video v from region r in time slot T
t_v	Average download time of a video per request
t_t	Length of a time slot
$f_{v,r}^T$	The binary value indicating whether video v is deployed in region r in time slot T or not
F_v^T	The deployment plan for video v in time slot T
$c_{i,r}$	The gain for a viewer in region i to download a video from region r
U_r	The upload bandwidth reserved in region r
L	The number of time slots for the upload reservation to be performed
P_r	The price for each unit of upload capacity in region r
W	The video service provider's budget for upload capacity purchase
$z_r(U_r)$	The gain for reserving U_r upload bandwidth in region r
$q_v(i, j, F_v^T)$	The estimated number of requests for video v from viewers in region i that will be sent to region j under the deployment plan F_v^T

3.3.2 View Number Predictability

To investigate the correlation between video link propagation on Weibo and the actual number of viewers in Youku, we study the following measurements in Weibo traces.

Number of Views and Number of Root Users. On Weibo, different users may introduce links to the same video on Youku from time to time, each of whom becomes a *root user* in this video's propagation. The more root users a video has, the more likely the video will attract more views in the future. With all of the samples that we

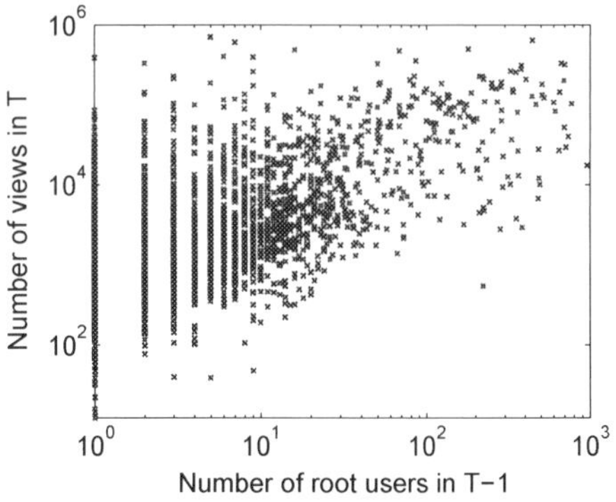

Fig. 3.2 The number of views vs. the number of root users in the previous time slot

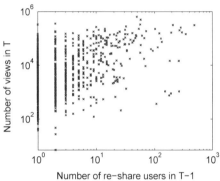

Fig. 3.3 The number of views vs. the number of re-share users in the previous time slot

collected, a Pearson's sample correlation coefficient [4] of 0.31 is computed from the pairs of the numbers of root users and the numbers of views with a lag of 1 time slot (in this chapter, each time slot is 4 h) for these videos, showing a positive correlation between the two quantities, as illustrated in Fig. 3.2.

Number of Views and Number of Re-share Users. Similarly, when more users are re-sharing (referred to as *re-share users*) the links to their followers, more views can be expected on Youku. We have computed a Pearson's sample correlation coefficient of 0.29 between the pairs of the numbers of re-share users and the numbers of views with a lag of 1 time slot. Again, a positive correlation is observed between the two quantities, as illustrated in Fig. 3.3.

Number of Views and Number of Influenced Users. The *influenced users* on Weibo (followers of root and re-share users of a video link, who can see the microblogs of the video) may likely become actual viewers on Youku themselves. Specifically, a Pearson's sample correlation coefficient of 0.15 is derived from the pairs the numbers of influenced users and the numbers of views with a lag of 1 time slot, as illustrated in Fig. 3.4.

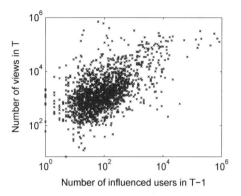

Fig. 3.4 The number of views vs. the number of influenced users in the previous time slot

3.3.3 Geographic Distribution Predictability

For video service deployment, we also need information about geographic distribution of viewers of different videos. Since Weibo users sharing a video link are "samples" of all viewers of that video on Youku, we investigate the geographic distribution of Weibo users who have published a microblog containing a link to the video and use it to estimate the distribution of all viewers in Youku. The rationale is that such microblogs are published by root and re-share users of the video, who may well have just viewed the video before posting on the microblogs. Our design in this chapter, however, is not limited to the Weibo sample of viewers' geographic distribution.

Given that the majority of viewers of Youku videos are in China, we consider 5 representative regions in China, namely BJ (Beijing), SH (Shanghai), SZ (Shenzhen), CD (Chengdu) and XA (Xi'an), where large CDNs in China commonly deploy data centers [28], and an overseas region, referred to as OS (overseas). We use $\mathscr{R}$ to denote the set of these regions, i.e., $\mathscr{R} = \{BJ, SH, SZ, CD, XA, OS\}$. We map the IP addresses of users in our Weibo traces to the six regions using an IP-to-location mapping database and estimate the geographic distribution of viewers of video v at time T by a 6-dimensional vector

$$G_v^T = \{r_v^{BJ}(T), r_v^{SH}(T), r_v^{SZ}(T), r_v^{CD}(T), r_v^{XA}(T), r_v^{OS}(T)\},$$

where $r_v^X(T)$ is the normalized fraction of Weibo microblogs containing links to video v, posted by users in region X in time slot T, and $r_v^{BJ}(T) + r_v^{SH}(T) + r_v^{SZ}(T) + r_v^{CD}(T) + r_v^{XA}(T) + r_v^{OS}(T) = 1$.

Skewed Geographic Distribution. Figure 3.5 plots the average fraction of microblogs posted in each region containing links to each of the videos, among all the microblogs posted for all videos in the ten-day trace span. We observe that the distribution over different regions is highly skewed: as much as 40% of viewers of over 50% of the videos reside in the Beijing and Shanghai regions, whereas

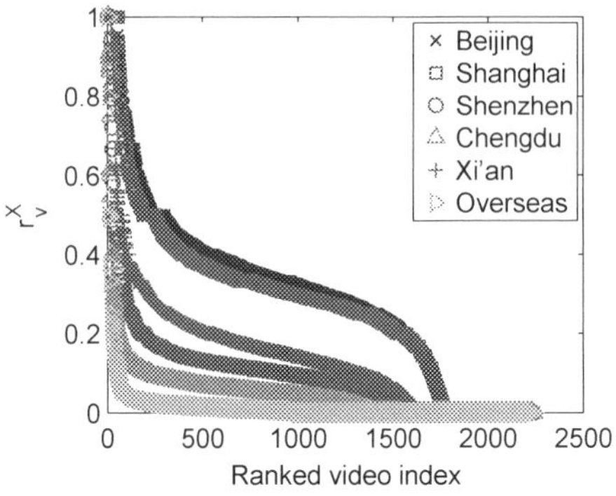

Fig. 3.5 Geographic distribution of Weibo users involved in propagation of different videos

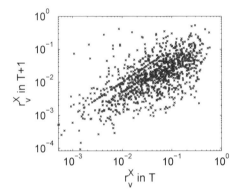

Fig. 3.6 Correlation between fractions of Weibo users in a region in two consecutive time slots

very small fractions of viewers are from overseas. This observation indicates that heterogeneous video service deployment is needed for different regions.

Predictability of the Future Geographic Distribution. To investigate whether future geographic distribution can be predicted using historical distributions, we plot in Fig. 3.6 the fraction of microblogs posted in a region in time slot T (i.e., $r_v^X(T)$, $X \in \mathscr{R}$) versus that in the previous time slot $T - 1$ (i.e., $r_v^X(T - 1)$) for each of the regions ($X \in \mathscr{R}$) and each of the videos ($v \in \mathscr{V}$). A positive correlation between the two can be observed, with a correlation coefficient of 0.29. This observation suggests that historical geographic distribution can potentially predict the future distribution.

3.3.4 Impact of Measures at Different Time Lags

Besides observing correlations between numbers of root/re-share/influenced users (resp. fraction of Weibo users of a video) in time $T - 1$ and Youku view numbers (resp. fraction of Weibo users of a video) at T, we further investigate the correlation

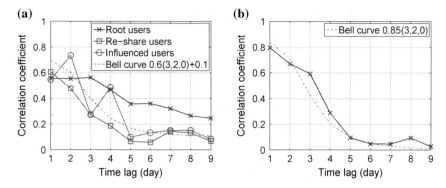

Fig. 3.7 Influence of the numbers of root/re-share/influenced users on the view number and geographic distribution at different time lags

at different time lags between the two. To avoid the impact of videos that are only viewed in a very short time span, we have selected 100 videos that have a relatively long popularity span; i.e., they were regularly viewed by users over 10 days.

First, for each of the 100 selected videos, we calculate the Pearson correlation coefficient between a 10-day series of the number of views of the video on Youku and a 10-day series of the number of root/re-share/influenced users of the video at different time lags between the two series. In Fig. 3.7a, each sample represents the average correlation coefficient over those of all videos, calculated at a specific time lag between the involved time series. We see that the correlation weakens as the time lag becomes larger, and the correlation coefficients are quite small when the lag is greater than 7 days. Hence, we will only use measurements collected in the previous 7 days for the prediction of view numbers.

Second, we plot in Fig. 3.7b the Pearson correlation coefficients between the fractions of a video's microbloggers in the six regions at T and those at different time lags, where each sample is the average over those of all 100 videos with data extracted from a 10-day interval. Similarly, recent geographic distributions have more influence on the future geographic distribution, which will be weighted more in our prediction model in Sect. 3.4.

3.4 Neural Network for View Prediction

When making video service deployment decisions, the video service provider is interested to know two things about a video in the near future: (1) Will the video attract more or fewer viewers such that more or fewer servers should be allocated to serve the video? (2) From which regions should servers be used to best satisfy these users from different locations?

3.4.1 Using Neural Networks for Prediction Models

In our design, we predict the number of views of a video, and the geographic distribution of the viewers, based on historical information from the microblogging system, using neural networks.

Merits of using neural networks. (1) Neural networks have been proven effective for time series prediction [2], as what we are pursuing. (2) According to our measurement study, the relationship between the number of root/re-share/influenced users and the number of Youku views can be non-linear. Neural networks are effective for learning such non-linear relationships [7].

The structure of the neural networks. In our study, we train two neural network models, (A) one for predicting the total number of views of a video and (B) the other for forecasting the geographic distribution of viewers. We use a 3-layer feed-forward neural network for both predictions, since it has been proven that multilayer neural networks with only one hidden layer are universal approximators [9]. In predicting video views, the structure of the neural network may remain for a relatively long time, but the training of the networks may take place frequently, using the new training dataset in the most recent time slots, as long as the video service provider has sufficient computational resources.

3.4.2 Constructing Input Features

To use the social measurements in Sect. 3.3 as input features, we need to determine a time window, a frequency for feature exaction in the time window (i.e., the number of time slots sampled in the time window), and the weight of each feature in the learning framework.

Time Window. We use a proper time window to avoid noisy features to be selected for the training. According to Sect. 3.3.4, the correlation between the number of Youku views and its influential Weibo measurements (i.e., the numbers of root/re-share/influenced users), in addition to the correlation between the geographic distribution of viewers and its influential measurements (i.e., the historical fraction of users residing in different regions), are weaker when the time lags are larger. Hence, we only extract features within the recent 7 days to train neural networks (A) and (B). For a newly published video with a lifetime shorter than 7 days, we use measurements throughout its past lifetime.

Frequency. The features are extracted from the following time slots: $T - 1, T - 7, T - 13, \ldots$, i.e., consecutive features are collected with a time interval of 24 h (recall that each time slot is 4 h), to capture the daily patterns. Let M denote the number of days the features are extracted.

Weight. Existing studies have shown that the learning performance of a neural network model can be improved by properly weighting the input features [21]. We weight the features from different time slots according to their levels of correlation with the prediction targets. In Fig. 3.7a, b, the curves of Pearson correlation coefficients can be fitted well by generalized bell functions $f(x) = \frac{e}{1+|\frac{x-c}{a}|^{2b}} + d$ (in Fig. 3.7, for simplicity, we denote a particular bell function by "$e(a, b, c) + d$"). Hence, we weight the number of root/re-share/influenced users, to be used as features in neural network (A), by $\alpha(x) = \frac{0.6}{1+|x/3|^4} + 0.1$, and the past geographic distributions of viewers, which are used as features in neural network (B), by $\beta(x) = \frac{0.85}{1+|x/3|^4}$, where x is the time lag between the time slots when the prediction target and the corresponding features happen.

In our design, we use $R_v^T(i)$, $S_v^T(i)$, and $I_v^T(i)$ to denote the number of root, re-share, and influenced users of video v in the ith time slot in the time window before T, respectively. We use $G_{v,r}^T(i)$ to denote the fraction of microblogs of video v posted by users in region r in the ith time slot in the time window before T.

Let X_v^T and Y_v^T be the features of the samples for training neural network (A) and neural network (B), respectively. We have $X_v^T = \{\alpha(i)R_v^T(i), \alpha(i)S_v^T(i), \alpha(i)I_v^T(i)|i = 1, 2, \ldots, M\}$ in neural network (A) and features $Y_v^T = \{\beta(i)G_{v,r}^T(i)|\forall r \in \mathcal{R}, i = 1, 2, \ldots, M\}$ in neural network (B).

3.4.3 Samples for Training and Evaluation

To train and evaluate the neural networks, we first pre-labeled samples from the traces, and each sample consists of the input features and the prediction target(s). In neural network (A), a sample is $\{X_v^T, \bar{V}_v^T\}$, where $\bar{V}_v^T$ is a vector that denotes the level of view number of video v in time slot T. Using the level of view number is sufficient for bandwidth allocation and can provide much better prediction accuracy than using the exact view number. According to the popularity distribution of the videos illustrated in Fig. 3.1a, we classify the number of views N for a video into 5 levels: (1) $N < 500$, (2) $500 \leq N < 5000$, (3) $5000 \leq N < 10,000$, (4) $10,000 \leq N < 100,000$, and (5) $N \geq 100,000$. $\bar{V}_v^T$ is a 5-dimensional binary vector with $\bar{V}_v^T[i] = 1$ and $\bar{V}_v^T[j] = 0, \forall j \neq i$, denoting that the number of views belongs to the ith level. The rationale of classifying the view numbers into different levels is that in video service deployment, the level of view numbers determines the bandwidth needed.

In contrast, in neural network (B), a sample is $\{Y_v^T, G_v^T\}$, where G_v^T is a 6-dimensional vector in which each element represents the fraction of microblogs of the video posted in one of the six regions in $\mathcal{R}$ in time slot T.

In summary, we have 35,000 samples for the neural network training and evaluation in total, corresponding to 1000 videos, covering both old videos and newly published ones. We randomly use 6,000 of them for the evaluation and the other 29,000 for the training process.

3.4.4 Training Neural Networks

Training Neural Network (A). The *output layer* in the neural network for predicting the number of views consists of 5 neurons, corresponding to the elements in vector $\bar{V}_v^T$, respectively. The *input layer* has $3M$ nodes, corresponding to the feature set X_v^T, i.e., $M = 7$ for old videos, and $M = 1, 2, \ldots, 6$ for new videos published M days ago. In the *hidden layer*, the number of neurons is decided as follows: we vary the number of hidden neurons from 15 to 25 and measure the number of samples whose view numbers can be classified into the correct levels using a validation set containing 25% of all samples from the training set (i.e., 7,250 samples out of 29,000). We observe that 15 hidden neurons can achieve the best results in cases of old videos with a lifetime longer than 7 days, and 18 hidden neurons are needed for most of the new videos.

    Training Neural Network (B). The output layer in the neural network for predicting the geographic distribution of viewers corresponds to the 6-dimensional vector G_v^T. The input layer corresponds to a $6M$-dimensional vector that contains M vectors of viewer geographic distributions (each element is the fraction of microbloggers of video v in each of the six regions) in the previous M days. To determine the number of neurons in the hidden layer, we measure the MSE (mean squared error) between the output geographic distribution vector and the actual geographic distribution vector. A smaller MSE indicates that the predicted geographic distribution vectors are more accurate, i.e., the differences between the actual geographic distribution vectors and them are smaller. Neural network (B) for geographic distribution prediction is trained using the same traces as used in training Neural network (A), and our training results indicate that 20 hidden neurons provide the best accuracy for old videos, whereas 35 hidden neurons are required for new videos. Next, we will evaluate the accuracy of both the neural network models.

3.4.5 Evaluating the Predication Accuracy

We evaluate the accuracy of our neural network models using the 6000 samples. We compare the accuracy of our neural networks with that of a linear regression approach [15], in which the parameters (i.e., γ, ε) in the linear model (i.e., $y = \gamma x + \varepsilon$), are calculated based on minimizing the squared error of the M samples—the view numbers or user geographic fractions (i.e., y) and time points (i.e., x) as used for training samples in our neural network models.

    Figure 3.8 shows the evaluation results. We observe that our neural network models achieve much better prediction accuracy than that achieved by the linear regression approach. In addition, the number of views and geographic distribution of old videos can be better forecasted than those of the new videos due to the fewer number of features in the learning framework for new videos. These results indicate that

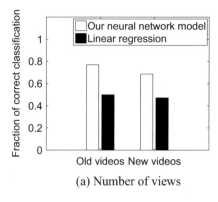
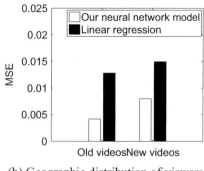

(a) Number of views   (b) Geographic distribution of viewers

Fig. 3.8 Prediction accuracy: a comparison

in today's social video sharing, using social information that reflects how videos are shared among users through social connections for predicting video popularity is promising.

3.5   Enhanced Video Service Deployment

3.5.1   Deployment Scheme and Objective

A distributed video service platform involves data centers in different geographic regions. In each data center, there is a shared storage backbone that stores the deployed videos and streaming servers that upload the videos to the requesting viewers. Better Internet connectivity and upload bandwidth can be achieved when a user downloads the video from a server located at a region that is close to the user [10].

The objective of our deployment algorithms is to proactively decide the total amount of upload bandwidth to reserve in each data center for this video service, which videos to be replicated in each data center at each time, and how to schedule the upload to viewers of different videos from different regions such that minimal video download delays are experienced by viewers throughout the entire system.

Let binary vector $F_v^T = \{f_{v,r}^T | \forall r \in \mathscr{R}\}$ denote the replication plan for video v in time slot T, where $f_{v,r}^T = 1$ indicates that video v is stored in region r in T and $f_{v,r}^T = 0$ otherwise. We use $c_{i,r}$ to denote the gain for a user in region i to download a video from servers in region r, which is calculated as the inverse proportion of the average delay between regions i and r, i.e., $c_{i,r} = \frac{1}{RTT(i,r)}$, where $RTT(i,r)$ is the average round-trip time (RTT) between the two regions (other gain function can also apply in our design, e.g., end-to-end bandwidth). When downloading a video, a viewer in region i first tries to request it from servers with the smallest RTT to achieve the largest gain. If servers in that region are not able to serve this request, the viewer's request is redirected to the next best region, until the request is eventually served. On the other hand, a streaming server serves all the requests when it has enough upload bandwidth; otherwise, it selects the requests to serve by prioritizing those from regions with small RTTs to the region where the server is located.

3.5.2 Regional Upload Bandwidth Reservation

The video upload bandwidth in each region is purchased from the respective Internet service providers. Let W denote the total budget that the video service provider is willing to spend on the upload capacity. We decide the amount of upload bandwidth to reserve in each region according to the average number of concurrent requests $V_r, \forall r \in \mathscr{R}$, and the unit prices $P_r, \forall r \in \mathscr{R}$, for upload bandwidth in different regions. Suppose that every video request is served by one unit upload bandwidth.

The upload bandwidth reservation in each region is performed every L time slots, considering the practice that bandwidth reservations are made for long periods in the real world. We compute V_r as the average number of concurrent requests from region r in the previous L time slots. We determine the bandwidth reservation by solving the following optimization problem:

$$\max_{\mathscr{U}} \sum_{r \in \mathscr{R}} z_r(U_r) \tag{3.1}$$

subject to:

$$\sum_{r \in \mathscr{R}} P_r U_r \leq W, \quad \text{and} \quad U_r \geq 0, \forall r \in \mathscr{R},$$

where $\mathscr{U} = \{U_r, \forall r \in \mathscr{R}\}$, and U_r is the upload capacity reserved in region r. $z_r(U_r)$ is the gain for reserving upload capacity U_r in region r. Suppose that $c_{r_0,r} \geq c_{r_1,r} \geq c_{r_2,r} \ldots \geq c_{r_{R-1},r}$, where $r_0 = r$ and $r_i \in \mathscr{R} \setminus \{r\}, i = 1, \ldots, R - 1$ (recall $c_{i,r} = \frac{1}{RTT(i,r)}$). $z_r(U_r)$ is defined as follows:

$$z_r(U_r) = \begin{cases} c_{r_0,r}U_r, & \text{if } 0 \leq U_r \leq V_{r_0}; \\ z_r(V_{r_0}) + c_{r_1,r}(U_r - V_{r_0}), & \text{if } V_{r_0} < U_r \leq V_{r_0} + V_{r_1}; \\ \ldots \\ z_r(\sum_{i=0}^{R-2} V_{r_i}) + c_{r_{R-1},r}(U_r - \sum_{i=0}^{R-2} V_{r_i}), \\ \quad \text{if } \sum_{i=0}^{R-2} V_{r_i} < U_r \leq \sum_{i=0}^{R-1} V_{r_i}; \\ z_r(\sum_{i=0}^{R-1} V_{r_i}), & \text{if } \sum_{i=0}^{R-1} V_{r_i} < U_r. \end{cases}$$

The rationale is as follows: when the reserved upload capacity in region r is no larger than the amount needed for serving all requests in the region, all the reserved bandwidth in r is to be used to serve only the requests from r, thereby achieving a gain of $c_{r,r}U_r$. When the reserved upload capacity in region r is more than that needed for serving this region, the extra bandwidth is used first to serve requests from region r_1 with the largest $c_{r_1,r}$ (i.e., smallest delay to r), thereby achieving an additional gain of $c_{r_1,r}(U_r - V_r)$; if there is further bandwidth left, it can be used to serve requests from region r_2, and so on.

We design Algorithm 4 to solve the optimal bandwidth reservation problem in (3.1). We always allocate a certain amount of upload bandwidth (Δ) to region r' with the current largest positive marginal gain per unit price $z'_r(U_r)/P_r$, where the marginal gain $z'_r(U_r)$ is derived as follows:

$$z'_r(U_r) = \begin{cases} c_{r_0,r}, & \text{if } 0 \le U_r \le V_{r_0}, \\ c_{r_1,r}, & \text{if } V_{r_0} < U_r \le V_{r_0} + V_{r_1}, \\ \dots \\ c_{r_{R-1},r}, & \text{if } \sum_{i=0}^{R-2} V_{r_i} < U_r \le \sum_{i=0}^{R-1} V_{r_i}, \\ 0, & \text{if } \sum_{i=0}^{R-1} V_{r_i} < U_r. \end{cases}$$

The amount of upload bandwidth to allocate to region r' is computed using $\Delta = \min(\sum_{i=0}^{k} V_{r'_i} - U_{r'}, W'/P_{r'})$, where $\sum_{i=0}^{k-1} V_{r'_i} \le U_{r'} < \sum_{i=0}^{k} V_{r'_i}$, and W' denotes the remaining budget. $r'_i, i = 0, 1, \dots$, are the series of regions such that $c_{r'_0,r'} \ge c_{r'_1,r'} \ge c_{r'_2,r'} \ge \dots$. Region k is the one selected from the ranked regions whose viewing requests are to be served by servers in region r' to achieve the largest gain. Then, we deduct $P_{r'}\Delta$ from the budget W' and repeat the allocation until all the budget is used up or the upload capacities allocated can already serve all the requests.

The complexity of Algorithm 4 depends on the number of regions to allocate the upload bandwidth resource to. In particular, the algorithm iteratively allocates the upload bandwidth to the "slots" in each region, where a slot represents the amount of bandwidth allocated in each iteration. Thus, the time complexity of this algorithm is $O(|\mathcal{R}|^2 \log |\mathcal{R}|)$, where $\log |\mathcal{R}|$ is a result of maintaining a heap structure for the ranking. Since there are only tens of regions deployed by a large video service provider, this algorithm can be executed effectively even in a centralized manner.

3.5.3 Video Replication

Next, we use the following heuristic algorithm to replicate videos to these regions, as summarized in Algorithm 5.

Predicting views using neural network models. The video service provider collects statistics from the online microblogging system, i.e., the number of root/re-share/influenced users and the geographic distribution of video microblogs in the previous M days, and estimates the level of views, $\bar{V}_v^T$, and the geographic distribution of views, $G_{v,r}^T$, of each video from each region in the next time slot using our

---

Algorithm 4 Upload bandwidth reservation for different regions (executed every L time slots)

1: **procedure** UPLOADALLOCATION(W, P_r, $c_{r_i,r}$, $i = 1, \ldots, R - 1, \forall r \in \mathscr{R}$)
2:    Update $V_r \forall r \in \mathscr{R}$ as the average number of concurrent video requests
3:    $U_r \leftarrow 0, \forall r \in \mathscr{R}$
4:    $W' \leftarrow W$
5:    **while** $W' > 0$ **and** $\exists r \in \mathscr{R}, z'_r(U_r) > 0$ **do**
6:       Choose the region r' with the largest $z'_r(U_r)/P_r$ among all the regions
7:       **if** $\exists k, \sum_{i=0}^{k-1} V_{r'_i} \leq U_{r'} < \sum_{i=0}^{k} V_{r'_i}$ **then**
8:          $\Delta \leftarrow \min(\sum_{i=0}^{k} V_{r'_i} - U_{r'}, W'/P_{r'})$
9:          $U_{r'} \leftarrow U_{r'} + \Delta$
10:         $W' \leftarrow W' - P_{r'}\Delta$
11:      **end if**
12:   **end while**
13: **end procedure**

---

proposed neural networks. Note that the neural network models are calibrated at the end of each time slot based on the newly collected view numbers and distribution.

Let $V_{v,r}^T$ denote the predicted number of concurrent video requests from region r for video v in time slot T, which is derived by $V_{v,r}^T = avg(\bar{V}_v^T)G_{v,r}^T \frac{t_v}{t_t}$, where $avg(\bar{V}_v^T)$ is the average number of views in output level $\bar{V}_v^T$. We assume that the video popularity is uniformly distributed in the popularity groups (1–4); the average number is then calculated as follows: $avg(1) = 250$, $avg(2) = 2750$, $avg(3) = 7500$, $avg(4) = 55000$, and for the last popularity group 5, we let $avg(5) = 150000$, where $avg(5)$ corresponds to videos with the number of views larger than 100000— there are very few videos with view number greater than 100000, and the average number is closer to 150000, as illustrated in Fig. 3.1a. t_v is the average service time for a request of video v and t_t is the time slot length ($t_v \ll t_t$, since t_v is generally a few minutes for short videos and t_t is 4 h). In doing so, we seek to use the number of concurrent video requests for bandwidth allocation (recall that each video request is served by one unit upload bandwidth).

Replicating videos to different regions. Let $q_v(i, j, F_v^T)$ denote the estimated number of concurrent viewing requests for video v from region i that will be sent to region j under replication plan F_v^T in T. According to the request service scheme discussed at the beginning of this section, $q_v(i, j, F_v^T)$ can be derived as follows:

$$q_v(i, j, F_v^T) = \begin{cases} 0, & \text{if } f_{v,j}^T = 0 \\ \begin{cases} 0 & f_{v,i}^T = 1, i \neq j \\ V_{v,i}^T & i = j \\ \frac{V_{v,i}^T}{\sum_{k \in \mathscr{R}} f_{v,k}^T} & f_{v,i}^T = 0 \end{cases} & \text{, if } f_{v,j}^T = 1 \end{cases}.$$

The rationale lies in the following: (1) if v is not deployed in j or v is deployed in i itself, where $i \neq j$, no request for video v from region i is to be sent to region j, i.e., $q_v(i, j, F_v^T) = 0$; (2) if $i = j$ and the video is deployed in region i (j), all requests are potentially served locally, i.e., $q_v(i, j, F_v^T) = V_{v,i}^T$; and (3) if v is not deployed in i but deployed in j, each region caching the video receives an equal share of the requests from i, assuming users' region preference is uniformly distributed, i.e., $q_v(i, j, F_v^T) = \frac{V_{v,i}^T}{\sum_{k \in \mathscr{R}} f_{v,k}^T}$. We calculate the gain of video v under a particular deployment plan F_v^T as follows:

$$B_v(F_v^T) = \sum_{r \in \mathscr{R}} \sum_{i \in \mathscr{R}} c_{i,r} q_v(i, r, F_v^T).$$

To determine whether a video should be replicated to a particular region, we evaluate the marginal gain $b_{v,r}$, which represents the potential improvement in video v's gain if v is to be deployed in region r:

$$b_{v,r} = B_v(F_v'^T) - B_v(F_v^T), \tag{3.2}$$

where $F_v'^T = \{f_{v,i}'^T | \forall i \in \mathscr{R}\}$, and $f_{v,i}'^T = \begin{cases} f_{v,i}^T, & i \neq r \\ 1, & i = r. \end{cases}$

We first initialize $F_v^T \leftarrow \{0, 0, \ldots\}, \forall v \in \mathscr{V}$, such that videos will be deployed according to their requests in the current time slot. Let $\mathscr{B} = \{b_{v,r} | \forall v \in \mathscr{V}, \forall r \in \mathscr{R}\}$, and sort $\mathscr{B}$ in descending order. To best utilize the reserved bandwidth U_r in each region r, each time we select a video-region pair with the largest $b_{v,r}$, deploy video v in region r in T (or retain video v in region r in T if it is already deployed) if r still has enough upload capacity to serve all the requests for the video that will be sent to r, and remove $b_{v,r}$ from $\mathscr{B}$. If v is deployed in r, $b_{v,l}, \forall l \in \mathscr{R}$ should be updated and $\mathscr{B}$ should be resorted. The steps are repeated until none of the regions has upload capacity left or there is no video-region candidate in set $\mathscr{B}$.

The complexity of Algorithm 5 depends on ranking $\mathscr{B}$ and maintaining the rank in lines 7–16. The time complexity is thus $O(|\mathscr{V}||\mathscr{R}| \log |\mathscr{V}||\mathscr{R}|) \sim O(|\mathscr{V}| \log |\mathscr{V}|)$, since $|\mathscr{R}| \ll |\mathscr{V}|$. The algorithm is sufficiently efficient when the candidate video set is small (e.g., the most recently published videos are to be deployed) and the deployment is not adjusted very frequently—we will evaluate the performance of the deployment by varying the execution interval in Sect. 3.6.

Algorithm 5 Video Deployment Based on Prediction.

1: **procedure** VIDEODEPLOYMENT($\bar{V}_v^T$, G_v^T, $\forall v \in \mathcal{V}$)
2:     Initialize $F_v^T \leftarrow \{0, 0, \ldots\}, \forall v \in \mathcal{V}$
3:     Calculate $b_{v,r}, \forall v \in \mathcal{V}, \forall r \in \mathcal{R}$, according to Eq. (3.2)
4:     $\mathcal{B} \leftarrow \{b_{v,r} | \forall v \in \mathcal{V}, \forall r \in \mathcal{R}\}$
5:     Sort $\mathcal{B}$ in descending order
6:     $Q(v, r, F_v^T) \leftarrow \sum_{i \in \mathcal{R}} q_v(i, r, F_v^T), \forall v \in \mathcal{V}, \forall r \in \mathcal{R}$
7:     **while** $\exists r, U_r > \sum_{v \in \mathcal{V}} Q(v, r, F_v^T)$ **and** $\mathcal{B} \neq \Phi$ **do**
8:         Pick the largest $b_{v,r}$ in the sorted order of $\mathcal{B}$
9:         $f'^T_{v,r} \leftarrow 1$
10:         **if** $U_r - \sum_{k \in \mathcal{V}} Q(k, r, F_v^T) \geq Q(v, r, F'^T_v)$ **then**
11:             $F_v^T \leftarrow F'^T_v$
12:             Update $b_{v,l}, \forall l \in \mathcal{R}$
13:             Re-sort $\mathcal{B}$ in descending order
14:         **end if**
15:         Remove $b_{v,r}$ from $\mathcal{B}$
16:     **end while**
17: **end procedure**

3.6   Evaluating the Video Service Performance

3.6.1   Setup of Trace-Driven PlanetLab Experiments

The setup of the trace-driven experiments based on PlanetLab is as follows.

- *Geo-distributed servers.* We implement our algorithms in C++ and deploy them on PlanetLab [8]. We use 5 PlanetLab nodes in China and 1 node in the US, corresponding to the regions studied. Each PlanetLab node acts as a video streaming server. This setting is only limited by the traces, and our design can scale when more regions are used in the prediction.
- *Video deployment and user requests.* We use the 1000 videos, as described in the measurement studies in Sect. 3.3. The length of each video is 10 min and the streaming rate is 600 Kbps. Each server is assigned a number of videos in each time slot to serve according to the deployment algorithms. A PlanetLab node also generates the requests from viewers in that region, which are sent to different regions according to the video service scheme discussed in Sect. 3.5.
- *Traces and parameters.* We emulate the actual video visits recorded in our Youku traces in each time slot and the geographic distribution of viewers from our Weibo traces. The video requests in each time slot are uniformly distributed in a time slot. The upload bandwidth prices in the regions are randomly assigned in the range of [0.5, 1.5] per MB, and the default budget for the deployment is 20,000. The parameter M is set as the same used in the prediction model (i.e., 7 for old videos and n for new videos published n days ago), and L is set to 6 such that the allocation is performed everyday.

- *Benchmark.* For benchmarking the performance, we measure the delay between the time a viewer issues a request and the time it receives the first 1,000 KB of the video stream, which is the typical size of the video data before a viewer starts the playback. This delay consists mainly of the RTT between the request and service regions, in addition to the queueing and processing delay at the server.

3.6.2 Experimental Results

3.6.2.1 An Overview of Performance Comparison

First, we compare the performance of different upload bandwidth reservation schemes: (1) our scheme given in Algorithm 4; (2) a random allocation scheme in which a small amount of upload bandwidth is progressively allocated to a randomly selected region until the total expense exceeds the budget; (3) a proportional allocation scheme in which each time, a small amount of upload bandwidth is allocated to a region selected randomly according to a probability that is proportional to the number of views in that region, i.e., more upload bandwidth is allocated to regions with more viewing requests. Under each upload bandwidth reservation scheme, the same video deployment algorithm (Algorithm 5) is employed.

In Fig. 3.9, we observe that our bandwidth reservation scheme can achieve much smaller delays for the viewers, given that not only the number of viewing requests in each region but also the user preference of different regions are incorporated in our design.

We also study the request load of these service regions under different upload reservation schemes. In Fig. 3.10, each sample represents the fraction of requests served by a region versus the region's rank. We observe that in our design, the request load is neither very uniformly distributed, as achieved by the random scheme, nor highly skewed, as in the proportional approach. Instead, our upload bandwidth allocation scheme supplies adequate bandwidth in each region that matches the number of requests in that region. The reason is that our reservation is based on the microblogging prediction framework, which provides a better estimation of future requests in a region than the proportional scheme.

3.6.2.2 Impact of Deployment Interval

The video deployment algorithm is performed periodically, but frequent changes of deployment may face potential challenges: (1) videos may need to be frequently replicated among regions, incurring migration bandwidth consumption; and (2) input features to the learning frameworks need to be collected frequently, thus incurring a heavy load on the online microblogging system. We evaluate the performance of the video service system when the video deployment is performed in different intervals. Figure 3.12 shows that for both our video deployment algorithm and the linear

Fig. 3.9 Comparison under
different upload bandwidth
reservation schemes

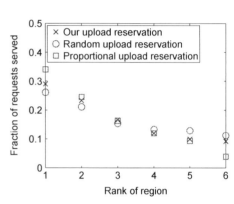

Fig. 3.10 Request load in
different regions

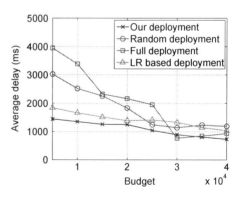

Fig. 3.11 Comparison under
different video deployment
schemes

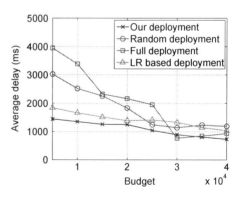

Fig. 3.12 Comparison for different deployment intervals

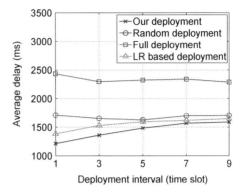

Fig. 3.13 Comparison between old and new videos

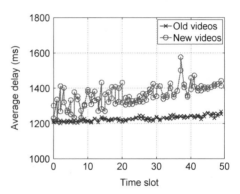

regression based scheme, the delay increases when the interval for deployment becomes larger, whereas for both the full replication and random deployment schemes, the delays remain at the same level regardless of the interval lengths. The results indicate that the deployment interval affects the performance of our design, and frequent adjustments of video deployment should be applied as long as the features from the online microblogging system can be collected in a timely manner.

3.6.2.3 Impact of Deployment Budget

We next compare our video deployment algorithm in Algorithm 5 with the following strategies: (1) a linear regression (LR)-based scheme, i.e., the same video service deployment algorithm but using the linear regression approach to predict the number and geographic distribution of video views; (2) a random deployment scheme, where each video is replicated in 1 randomly selected region in each time slot; (3) a full deployment scheme, where each video is replicated to all 6 regions. As for upload bandwidth reservation, we use the same scheme as in Algorithm 4 but under different budgets. In Fig. 3.11, we observe that our video deployment algorithm performs much better than the other schemes, especially when the budget is small. When the budget is larger than 25,000, which is approximately sufficient for purchasing bandwidth to serve all requests locally, all the schemes achieve similar delays. The observation indicates that compared with other schemes, our algorithm works effectively for a larger range of deployment budgets, since it more precisely deploy videos to a region with enough bandwidth, where they will be requested by many users in that region; in contrast, in the other deployment schemes, many viewing requests are redirected to regions without sufficient bandwidth capacity, thus resulting in large delays.

3.6.2.4   Impact of the Prediction Accuracy

We compare the delays at viewers of old videos and new videos, respectively, which are treated differently in the prediction frameworks. Figure 3.13 shows that viewers of old videos experience smaller delays than those of new videos. This is consistent with our evaluation results for the prediction accuracy in Sect. 3.4.5—better deployment performance can be achieved with videos having a larger feature window, where the prediction accuracy is higher. Because the prediction accuracy directly determines the video service deployment performance in our design, exploring new features from the microblogging services to improve the prediction accuracy is an approach to enhance the streaming quality for video sharing sites.

References

1. V.K. Adhikari et al., Reverse engineering the youtube video delivery cloud, in *IEEE Hot Topics in Media Delivery Workshop* (2011)
2. E.M. Azoff, *Neural Network Time Series Forecasting of Financial Markets* (Wiley, 1994)
3. M. Arlitt, B. Krishnamurthy, P. Gill, A few chirps about twitter, in *ACM Workshop on Online Social Networks (WOSN)* (2008)
4. J. Benesty et al., Pearson correlation coefficient, in *Noise Reduction in Speech Processing*? (Springer, 2009), pp. 291–324
5. M. Cha, A. Mislove, K.P. Gummadi, A measurement-driven analysis of information propagation in the Flickr social network, in *ACM International Conference on World Wide Web (WWW)* (2009)
6. M. Cha et al., I tube, you tube, everybody tubes: analyzing the world's largest user generated content video system, in *ACM SIGCOMM* (2007), pp. 1–14
7. S. Chen, S.A. Billings, P.M. Grant, Non-linear system identification using neural networks. Int. J. Control **51**(6), 1191–1214 (1990)
8. B. Chun et al., Planetlab: an overlay testbed for broad-coverage services. ACM SIGCOMM Comput. Commun. Rev. **33**(3), 3–12 (2003)
9. K. Hornik, M. Stinchcombe, H. White, Multilayer feedforward networks are universal approximators. Neural Netw. **2**(5), 359–366 (1989)
10. R. Krishnan et al., Moving beyond end-to-end path information to optimize CDN performance, in *ACM Internet Measurement Conference (IMC)* (2009)
11. H. Kwak et al., What is twitter, a social network or a news media?, in *ACM International Conference on World Wide Web (WWW)* (2010)
12. K. Lai, D. Wang, Towards understanding the external links of video sharing sites: measurement and analysis, in *ACM Network and Operating System Support for Digital Audio and Video (NOSSDAV)* (2010)

13. H. Li, H. Wang, J. Liu, Video sharing in online social network: measurement and analysis, in *ACM Network and Operating System Support for Digital Audio and Video (NOSSDAV)* (2012)
14. Y. Liu, Y. Guo, C. Liang, A survey on peer-to-peer video streaming systems. Peer-to-peer Netw. Appl. **1**(1), 18–28 (2008)
15. G.I. Marchuk, *Numerical Methods and Applications* (CRC, 1994)
16. R.H. Myers et al., *Generalized Linear Models* (Wiley, 2010)
17. G. Peng, CDN: content distribution network, in *arXiv preprint cs/0411069* (2004)
18. J. Ritterman, M. Osborne, E. Klein, Using prediction markets and twitter to predict a swine flu pandemic, in *1st International Workshop on Mining Social Media* (2009)
19. N. Savage, Twitter as medium and message. Commun. ACM **54**(3), 18–20 (2011)
20. M. Saxena, U. Sharan, S. Fahmy, Analyzing video services in web 2.0: a global perspective, in *ACM Network and Operating System Support for Digital Audio and Video (NOSSDAV)* (2008)
21. D.F. Specht, A general regression neural network. IEEE Trans. Neural Netw. **2**(6), 568–576 (1991)
22. G. Szabo, B.A. Huberman, Predicting the popularity of online content. Commun. ACM **53**(8), 80–88 (2010)
23. Z. Wang et al., Guiding internet-scale video service deployment using microblog-based prediction, in *IEEE International Conference on Distributed Computing Systems (INFOCOM)* (2012)
24. Z. Wang et al., Propagation-based social-aware replication for social video contents, in *ACM International Conference on Multimedia (Multimedia)* (2012)
25. I.H. Witten, E. Frank, M.A. Hall, *Data Mining: Practical Machine Learning Tools and Techniques* (Morgan Kaufmann, 2011)
26. D. Xu et al., Analysis of a CDN-P2P hybrid architecture for cost-effective streaming media distribution. Multimedia Syst. **11**(4), 383–399 (2006)
27. J. Yang, S. Counts, Predicting the speed, scale, and range of information diffusion in twitter, in *International AAAI Conference on Weblogs and Social Media* (2010)
28. H. Yin et al., Design and deployment of a hybrid CDN-P2P system for live video streaming: experiences with livesky, in *ACM International Conference on Multimedia (Multimedia)* (2009)

Chapter 4
Propagation-Based Social Video Content Replication

Abstract Content propagates across the social connections between people in the online social network. The propagation patterns affect how content reaches different users, making it promising to deploy content according to the social propagation. This chapter explores strategies for using propagation patterns to perform content replication for social content delivery.

Keywords Content replication · Social propagation · Propagation patterns · Request locality

4.1 Introduction

Recent years have witnessed the blossom of online social network service (e.g., Facebook, Twitter) and online content sharing service (e.g., YouTube, Flickr), in addition to the rapid convergence of both services. *Social multimedia content*, or *social content* in short, that is *generated* and *shared* by users in online social networks is becoming increasingly popular on today's Internet. ForeSee has reported that more than 18% users are influenced by the social network when accessing online video content. It is fascinating to study how social content can be served to users with satisfactory Quality-of-Experience (QoE).[1]

In an online social network, users create and maintain different social connections, e.g., *friending* their friends in real life, *following* celebrities or even *liking* virtual social entities. Such social connections determine how shared content can reach users in the online social network [16]. The unique *propagation* properties make the content access pattern in the online social network quite different from that in the traditional centralized content sharing systems, in that (1) content is no longer produced by a few centralized content providers but rather by all individual users and (2) social connections and social activities determine the propagation of content among users.

---

[1] ©[2013] IEEE. Reprinted, with permission, from ACM Transactions on Multimedia Computing, Communications, and Applications.

© The Author(s) 2018
Z. Wang et al., *Online Social Media Content Delivery*,
SpringerBriefs in Computer Science, https://doi.org/10.1007/978-981-10-2774-1_4

We are facing the following challenges in distributing the social contents with satisfactory QoE: (1) a significant amount of user-generated content (UGC) requires a large amount of storage and network resource, e.g., YouTube has hit a new record of 72 h worth of videos uploaded by users per minute; (2) newly generated content tends to attract most of the users, but it is difficult to estimate its popularity for service allocation, which is dynamically affected by the social network [5]; (3) social content has close-to-uniform [21] and highly-volatile popularity profiles because a large portion of the content is shared among small social groups (e.g., family members).

Challenge (1) makes traditional service paradigms (e.g., C/S based on private servers) not suitable—it is too expensive to replicate all content to all servers, and a common practice to provision these content services is to replicate content to severs at different geographic regions [2] by allocating resource from the geo-distributed CDN (Content Delivery Network) or cloud, where content can be dynamically placed to serve users all over the world. Challenges (2) and (3) make the traditional replication approaches, which work well only for content with skewed and stable popularity profiles and are not suitable in the context of online social networks. Mislove et al. [23] have observed a large deduction in the cache hit ratio when traditional caching schemes are used to replicate social content.

Our preliminary study [30] reveals a key observation that social content, unlike regular content, does not propagate among users randomly—instead, it propagates along the social-network topology according to several rules determined by the social propagation. We now significantly extend our study to design a general framework with propagation patterns and predictions incorporated, based on which we develop a socially aware delivery system to effectively distribute social content with superb QoE. In this chapter, we use the most representative type of multimedia content— the social video content to study how the social content can be effectively replicated based on social propagation—but our design can be used in the delivery of a variety of multimedia types.

First, we demonstrate that the statistic information obtained from online social networks can guide the video replication. We conduct large-scale measurement studies to explore the connection between social propagation and replication and discover the propagation patterns of social video contents, including social locality that videos are generally shared among users who are socially connected, geographical locality that most of the videos are shared between users that are geographically close to each other, and temporal locality that newly published videos can attract most of the viewers.

Second, based on the propagation patterns, we design propagation predictors to guide the content delivery. In particular, the propagation region predictor, global-audience predictor and local-audience predictor answer the following questions, respectively: (a) which videos should be replicated to which edge-cloud servers? (b) how much bandwidth should be reserved for each video by the edge-cloud? and (c) which videos should be served by which peers?

Third, based on the propagation patterns (i.e., localities in propagation), we propose a propagation-based social content distribution framework, in which a hybrid edge-cloud [34] and peer-assisted video replication architecture is employed. Based on the propagation predictions, videos are replicated by both the edge-cloud servers and peers at different geographic locations as follows: (1) we design the edge-cloud replication strategies according to the region predictor and global-audience predictor, determining the region selection and bandwidth reservation; (2) we further design the peer-assisted replication according to the local-audience predictor, performing socially aware cache replacement at each peer.

The remainder of this chapter is organized as follows. In Sect. 4.2, we discuss related work. In Sect. 4.3, we motivate our design by measurement studies on social content propagation. We present the propagation pattern-based architecture in Sect. 4.4 and the detailed replication strategies based on propagation predictions in Sect. 4.5. In Sect. 4.6, we evaluate the performance of our design by trace-driven experiments. In Sect. 4.7, we discuss some implementation issues.

4.2 Related Work

4.2.1 Propagation in Online Social Networks

Online social networks have become a popular type of Internet service. Based on traces from Flickr, LiveJournal and Orkut, Mislove et al. [22] study the topology of the social graph and confirm the power-law, small-world, and scale-free properties of online social networks. Krishnamurthy et al. [3] investigate Twitter and identify the distinct classes of Twitter users and their behaviors, in addition to the geographic growth patterns of the social network.

In an online social network, content spreads among users by their social activities. A number of research efforts have been devoted to studying the propagation of information in online social networks. Kwak et al. [16] investigate the impact of users' retweets on information diffusion in Twitter. Dodds et al. [9] use the epidemic model to study the information propagation, where a piece of information is regarded as an infective disease that spreads via the social connections. Kempe et al. [15] investigate how to maximize the spread of influence in an online social network, and Hartline et al. [12] utilize such maximum spread to achieve revenue maximization, i.e., the largest number of buyers can be attracted by selecting the best set of initial users to push the information onto. Domingos et al. [10] explore the value of social networks in estimating potential buyers of a product or a service, which can be influenced by an existing customer.

In this chapter, we will study how to connect the social propagation and the social multimedia content replication, i.e., how statistical information about the content propagation can be utilized to guide the content replication.

4.2.2 Social Content Replication

Many architectures have been proposed in large-scale content service systems, including (1) the server-based architecture, e.g., CDN and cloud-based approaches

[25], (2) the client-based architecture, e.g., the P2P content distribution [18], and (3) the hybrid architecture, e.g., a hybrid CDN and P2P distribution framework [33]. For Internet-scale social content service, replicating the content at different geographic regions is a promising approach to provide good service quality to users [1]. Zhu et al. [34] propose allocating cloud servers at the network edges to distribute the multimedia contents to users.

Content-based replication. From the content aspect, traditional content distribution mainly takes content popularity into account, and allocates storage and bandwidth resource according to the popularity [14]. After 2005, a very large amount of content has been generated by users. Exploring the correlation between contents can effectively help users fetch content precisely [8]. However, online social networks have greatly changed the assumptions in traditional replication algorithms [4], e.g., the distribution of content has shifted from a "central-edge" manner to an "edge-edge" manner, resulting in a close-to-uniform popularity distribution. Li et al. [17] study content sharing in online social networks and observe the skewed popularity distribution of contents and the power-law activity of users. To better serve such social contents, some socially aware content replication schemes have been proposed.

Social-based replication. After online social network is widely used by people to access online content. User relation and influence are studied to reflect that after a content is shared by a person, it may be requested by his friends, such that contents can be distributed based on this inference. Pujol et al. [26] investigate the difficulties of scaling online social networks and design a social partition and replication middle-ware in which users' friends' data can be co-located in the same server. Tran et al. [28] study the partition of contents in the online social network by taking social relationships into consideration. Nguyen et al. [24] study how to improve the system efficiency in case of server failures by taking social locality into consideration. Wang et al. [29] observe that a social network can be used to help predict the content access pattern in a standalone on-demand system. Wu et al. [32] study how to minimize the cost in social media migration among servers at different regions. Cheng et al. [7] study the social media partition to balance the server load and preserve the social relationship.

Understanding the content access patterns is a key to perform effective content replication. With respect to understanding how users access content in online social networks, related works have been considering content and users separately. However, content sharing is dynamically determined by both the content and users. In order to address the problem of providing effective content distribution to users in the social network, we propose propagation-based social content distribution. This chapter is an extension of our preliminary studies in [30]—we design a new general framework for propagation-based social content delivery, incorporating both the propagation patterns and propagation predictions.

4.3 Measurement of Social Content Propagation

In this section, we present the logic framework of our study, our measurement setup and a glance of the propagation of social multimedia contents.

4.3.1 Framework

Figure 4.1 illustrates the logical framework of our design. (1) *Input.* User, content and context information is the input to our design. In particular, we use the social relationships and influences among users, their preferences in different contents, the content popularity and the server and user regional distributions to determine which users prefer to receive content from which servers. (2) *Propagation pattern mining.* Based on the input, we have observed the propagation patterns, including the social locality, geographical locality and temporal locality. (3) *Propagation prediction.* Based on these propagation patterns, we further design predictors for the propagation regions (i.e., where a video will be shared), the global audience (i.e., the global popularity of a video), and the local audience (i.e., how a video is shared between friends). (4) *Propagation-based replication.* Our replication architecture and strategies are designed according to the propagation patterns and the propagation predictions, respectively. Edge-cloud servers and peers are allocated to strategically serve the content such that users can download from the local servers.

4.3.2 Measurement Setup

In our measurement, we have collected traces from Tencent Weibo, which is a microblogging website via which users can broadcast a message including at most 140 characters to their friends. We obtained Weibo traces from the technical team of Tencent containing valuable runtime data of the system in 20 days (October 9–October 29) in 2011. Each entry in the traces corresponds to one

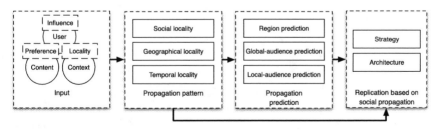

Fig. 4.1 Logical framework

Fig. 4.2 Connection between an online social network and a content sharing system

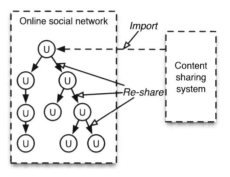

microblog posted, including the ID, name, IP address, geographic location of the publisher, time stamp when the microblog is posted, IDs of the parent and root microbloggers if it is a re-post, and contents of the microblog. The traces were recorded on an hourly basis.

We focus on microblogs with video links that are imported from external video sharing websites. In particular, we collected 350,860 video links from 5 popular video sharing sites: Youku, Ku6, Tudou, Xunlei and Tencent Video. We then retrieved the microblogs that are related to these video links, i.e., the microblogs either include the video links to these videos in their content or they are re-shares of the ones that include the links. These video links cover 1,923,507 microblogs in the time span, which are posted or re-shared by 1,465,328 users, from more than 200 regions in the propagation (each region is defined by Tencent as a geographical area). We also retrieve the profiles of users who have posted these microblogs, e.g., their friend lists. In our measurement, we use the number of microblog posts to estimate the number of video views, in a sense that the microblog publishers can represent a sample of users who have watched the videos.

Figure 4.2 illustrates how Tencent Weibo are connected with the video sharing sites. After a video is published on a video sharing site, the link to that video can be imported by users to Weibo. We regard the import as the video generation by that user. Then users who are socially connected to that user can be reached by the imported video and further re-share the video.

4.3.3 A Glance at the Generation, Distribution and Popularity of Social Content

Content Generation and Distribution. On Tencent Weibo, users generate videos by importing the links to the videos from the external video sharing sites and distribute the videos by re-sharing the microblogs containing the links. Importing and re-sharing are the most important activities that determine how videos reach users in an online social network. Figure 4.3 illustrates the number of imports and re-shares

Fig. 4.3 Imports and
re-shares over time

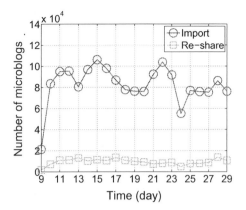

of the targeted videos over time. We observe that (1) more users are generating videos instead of distributing them in an online social network, and (2) the number of imports exhibits a more obvious weekly pattern than the number of re-shares, indicating more randomness in users' re-sharing of social video content.

Popularity Profiles. Videos can reach many people in an online social network by users' importing and re-sharing, which determine the video propagation range. We observe that different videos attract quite different levels of imports and re-shares, resulting in a skewed popularity distribution of videos in the online social network. We study the popularity distribution of social video content in terms of their imports and re-shares in a given time period of 1 day. In Fig. 4.4, videos are ranked in their import number's descending order. Each sample illustrates the number of imports of a video versus the rank of that video. We observe that the video import popularity is highly skewed, following a Zipf-like distribution with a shape parameter of $s = 0.8906$. Similarly, Fig. 4.5 illustrates the number of re-shares versus the rank of the video, and we observe that the video re-share popularity also follows a Zipf-like distribution with a shape parameter of $s = 0.9519$. The popularity distributions

Fig. 4.4 Number of imports
of a video versus its rank

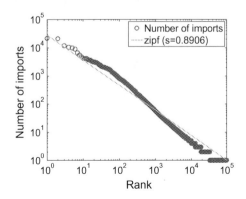

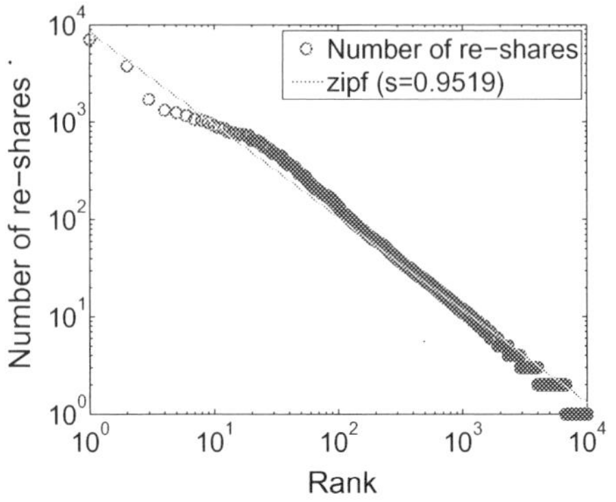

Fig. 4.5 Number of
re-shares of a video versus
its rank

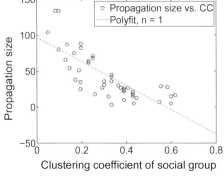

Fig. 4.6 Propagation size
versus the social group
clustering coefficient

of the imports and re-shares indicate that there is a dominant fraction of unpopular videos in the online social network—it is a great challenge to serve all of the videos to users locally; (e.g., users can download the videos from the servers located at the same region) with limited storage and network resources.

Social groups. We further investigate in which types of social groups these unpopular videos are propagating. By randomly collecting 50 videos with different propagation size (the number of users involved in a video's propagation), we explore the correlation between the propagation size and the clustering coefficient of the social group formed by the users involved in the propagation. In Fig. 4.6, each sample illustrates the video propagation size versus the clustering coefficient of the corresponding social group [31]. We observe a relatively strong correlation between the propagation size and the clustering coefficient. The reason is that the unpopular videos tend to be shared among small social groups that are relatively closely-connected (socially). The trend of many unpopular videos to be shared among small social groups results in a close-to-uniform popularity distribution, which makes the replication extremely challenging.

4.4 Replication Architecture Based on Propagation Patterns

In this section, we first present the propagation patterns observed in the measurement studies. Then, we present the architecture of our design and its key components based on the propagation patterns.

4.4.1 Social Propagation Patterns

We study the patterns of the social content propagation to guide our social content delivery architecture design.

4.4.1.1 Social Locality

The generation and re-sharing of a video on Weibo form a propagation tree that is rooted by the user who generates the video. Any user who re-shares the video becomes a new leaf node in the propagation tree. Figure 4.7 shows the propagation size of videos in 5 different categories. Each sample illustrates the number of propagation trees (with the same propagation size) versus the size of these propagation trees. We observe that the size of most propagation trees is very small; e.g., the sizes of more than 90% of the propagation trees are less than 100.

Next, we study the propagation depth, which is defined as the average number of social hops between users in the propagation tree and the root user. Figure 4.8 illustrates the propagation depth of videos in the same 5 categories. Each sample represents the number of propagation trees (with the same propagation depth) versus their propagation depth. We observe that in most of the propagation trees, the depth does not exceed 10; i.e., users who re-share the same video are socially close to the root user (with a small number of social hops between them).

Fig. 4.7 Number of propagation trees versus the propagation size

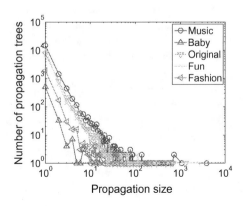

Fig. 4.8 Number of
propagation trees versus the
propagation depth

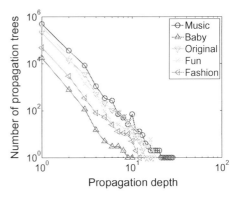

The limited propagation size and propagation depth indicate that in each propagation tree, only users within a *limited social range* will be reached by the video. This observation motivates us to design the peer-assisted replication such that users who are both socially and geographically close to each other can help distribute video content among themselves effectively.

4.4.1.2 Geographical Locality

Users who generate, re-share and view social videos are located in a variety of regions throughout the world. For Internet-scale video service providers, when performing replication for the social video contents, they need to strategically determine the regions (where datacenters are deployed) where the videos should be stored and served. To this end, we investigate how social video content propagates among different geographic regions.

First, we observe that the popularity of different regions is quite different. We define the import number of a region as the number of total imports issued by users in the region. In Fig. 4.9, we rank 41 regions in their import number's descending order. Each sample in this figure illustrates the import number of a region versus the rank of the region. We observe that the popularity distribution of regions with respect to their import numbers follows a logarithm function $y = 150000 - 35000 \log(1.443x)$. This observation indicates that it is not necessary to replicate each video to all the regions. A video should be replicated to a region only when the region is in the video's propagation range.

Second, we observe that most of the content propagates in a very small number of regions. In Fig. 4.10, each sample represents the number of regions involved in a content's propagation versus the rank of the content. We observe that most of the videos are shared by users from only a very few number of regions. More than 90% of the contents are propagating in less than 5 regions. This indicates that in social video sharing, users in a video's propagation can be geographically close to each other.

Fig. 4.9 Import number of a region versus the rank of the region

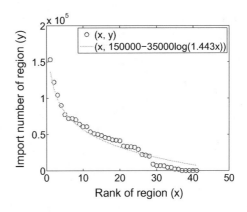

Fig. 4.10 Number of regions involved versus the rank of content

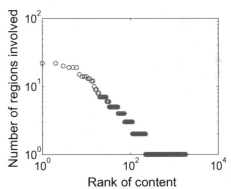

4.4.1.3 Temporal Locality

In the online social network, we observe that users are more likely to re-share new video content, i.e., videos that are recently imported or re-shared. Figure 4.11 illustrates the number of re-shares of a video in a timeslot (1 h) versus the time lag since the propagation tree is generated. We observe that most of the re-shares happen in the recent hours, and the re-share number against the time lag follows a Zipf-like distribution with a shape parameter $s = 1.5070$. More than 95% of the re-shares happen within the first 24 h. This indicates that in social video sharing, users' behaviors are highly crowded around the time point when a video is imported. We will also incorporate the temporal locality into our design.

4.4.2 Edge-Cloud and Peer-Assisted Replication Architecture

According to our observations, users in a video propagation are socially and geographically close to each other, and their social actions are clustered within a short

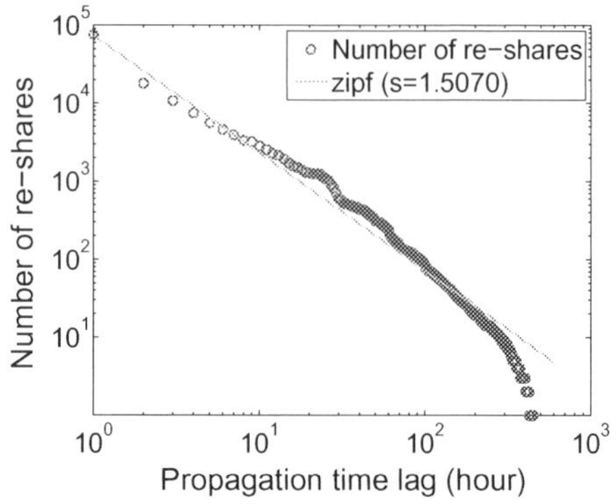

Fig. 4.11 Number of
re-shares versus the time lag

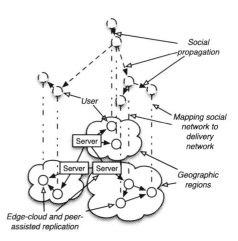

Fig. 4.12 Conceptual
architecture of PSAR

time period. Accordingly, we propose to use a *hybrid edge-cloud and peer-assisted* architecture for social video distribution, where the edge-cloud can support the time-varying bandwidth and storage allocations requested by different regions, whereas the peers are able to help contribute to each other in similar social groups. Figure 4.12 illustrates the conceptual architecture of our design. In this figure, two overlays are presented as follows: (1) *social propagation overlay* based on the social graph, which determines the video propagation among friends, i.e., after generating a video, users can share the video with their direct friends, who will further re-share the video to more people, and (2) *delivery overlay*, which determines how video content is delivered from edge-cloud servers to users or among themselves in a P2P paradigm. In this architecture, on one hand, we make use of the edge-cloud servers distributed in different geographic regions to serve the social videos to users from different regions; on the other hand, we let peers cache the video contents in their local storage such that they can help each other download the videos. In the design of *PSAR* (Propagation-Based Socially Aware Replication for social content), we will study the edge-cloud replication on how videos are replicated to edge-cloud servers, in addition to the peer-assisted replication on how videos are cached by a peer.

4.4.2.1 Edge-Cloud Replication

In the edge-cloud video replication, video content is generally replicated to servers located in different geographic regions. The main purpose of edge-cloud replication is for users at different locations to download the desired videos from their local servers, which are located in the same regions with the users, to improve the video service quality [1].

We redesign the edge-cloud replication by taking the social propagation into account. We first select the videos that are the most likely to propagate across geographic regions by evaluating the videos' geographic influence index we design. Since the selected videos are more likely to attract users from more regions in the future, we replicate them to more regions so that users can be better served by the local servers. Subsequently, based on the local-audience index, which reflects their popularity in the near future, we determine which regions to replicate these videos to and how much bandwidth to allocate for the videos. We will present the detailed design in Sect. 4.5.2.

4.4.2.2 Peer-Assisted Replication

The reason that we propose a joint edge-cloud and peer-assisted paradigm in the social video replication is two-fold: (1) social videos are generally shared in small social groups, resulting in the close-to-uniform popularity distribution of the videos, which causes a significant amount of server resource to be distributed to users. To scale the delivery system, peers' resources are in demand. (2) Users typically share videos with their friends who lie geographically close to each other [27]—these socially connected users tend to have good Internet connectivity between each other to perform the peer-assisted video downloads [13].

In traditional peer-assisted video distribution, LRU- and LFU-based cache replacement algorithms are widely used. Such algorithms only depend on the static popularity of the video content and thus cannot achieve good performance when the access patterns of videos are affected by the social activities in the online social network. Based on the local-audience index summarized from the propagation pattern, we redesign the peer cache replacement algorithm. In particular, we let peers cache videos that not only improve the general peer contribution (i.e., the fraction of video content uploaded by peers over all videos uploaded) but also improve the possibility for peers to serve the unpopular videos to their local friends. These friend users can benefit from the good Internet connectivity to the local peers. We will present the detailed design in Sect. 4.5.2.3.

4.5   Replication Strategies Based on Propagation Prediction

In this section, we first present the design challenges in PSAR. Then, we establish the connection between the social video propagation and the video replication using the propagation prediction. Subsequently, we present the detailed design of PSAR based on the connection.

Challenges in the Design of PSAR. In PSAR, the replication of social video contents is facing great resource-allocation challenges in the presence of multiple video propagations. Figure 4.13 illustrates an example when there are only two videos. In this figure, the circles represent users in the online social network, which are located in different geographic regions, e.g., region 1 and region 2. User A generates and shares video a in timeslot T, and then the video is re-shared by his friends C and D in timeslot $T + 1$. At the same time, another user B generates a different video b. Video a and video b will propagate across the social connections, and the two propagation trees may intersect in the same region or at the same peer, e.g., both region 1 and region 2 are involved in the two propagation trees, and both videos can reach user K in timeslot $T + 3$. The resource allocation has to determine (1) how to serve video a and b by the edge-cloud servers in region 1 and 2 and (2) how to cache videos a and b at the peers to help others. It is a great challenge when many videos are propagating at the same time. The two problems will be addressed when discussing the edge-cloud and peer-assisted replication methods.

4.5.1   Propagation Prediction

4.5.1.1   Propagation Region Prediction

Based on the dataset used in our measurement studies, Fig. 4.15 illustrates the correlation between the number of regions involved in the video propagation and the propagation size for different videos. We observe that a large propagation size generally results in more regions involved in the propagation. The relationship follows

Fig. 4.13 Resource allocation for two propagation trees

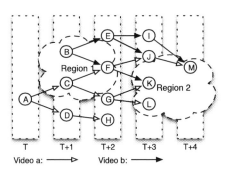

a logarithm function. In PSAR, the propagation size is utilized to determine whether a video will be replicated to more regions. In particular, we design a geographic influence index as follows:

$$g_v^{(T)} = c_1 \log(c_2 s_v^{(T-1)}),$$

where $s_v^{(T-1)}$ is the propagation size of the propagation tree of video v in timeslot $T - 1$. Large $g_v^{(T)}$ indicates that more regions will be involved in the propagation of the video. Intuitively, a video should be replicated to more regions when the predicted number of regions involved in the propagation is greater than the number of regions that it has already been replicated to.

4.5.1.2   Global-Audience Prediction

To allocate bandwidth to serve social video content, we design a global-audience predictor based on a global-audience index to evaluate the strength of a video's propagation in timeslot T, using the propagation information as follows: (1) the current propagation size $(s_v^{(T)})$, (2) the current propagation depth $(h_v^{(T)})$, and (3) the time lag since the propagation tree is formed $(\tau_v^{(T)})$. The global-audience index is defined as follows:

$$e_v^{(T)} = z_s(\tau_v^{(T)})(s_v^{(T)}/h_v^{(T)}),$$

where $z_s(\tau_v^{(T)})$ is a decreasing function to make use of the temporal locality, which can adjust the global-audience index according to $\tau_v^{(T)}$ such that more recently generated or shared videos will have a larger global-audience index. Based on our observation in Sect. 4.4.1.3, $z_s(t)$ is defined as follows:

$$z_s(t) = 1/(t^s \sum_{k=1}^{N} \frac{1}{k^s}),$$

where s is the Zipf shape parameter and N is the number of hours between the publication time of the earliest video and the publication time of the latest video. In our design, $e_v^{(T)}$ is used to guide the replication. Larger $e_v^{(T)}$ indicates that more users can join the propagation tree in timeslot T. The rationale of $e_v^{(T)}$ lies as follows: (1) larger $s_v^{(T)}$ indicates that more users can be reached by the video, and these users are the potential viewers (downloaders) of video v; (2) according to the social locality, small $h_v^{(T)}$ indicates that users in the propagation tree are still socially close to the root user and the video can reach more users; (3) according to the temporal locality, large $\tau_v^{(T)}$ slows down the propagation. Based on the global-audience index, we determine how much bandwidth we should reserve for a video in future timeslots in PSAR.

Figure 4.14 compares our socially aware global-audience prediction and the traditional popularity estimation using only the historical popularity. The effectiveness of

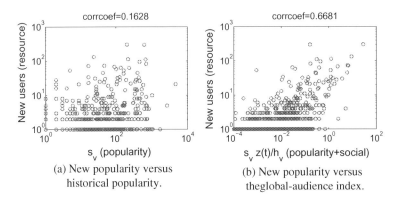

Fig. 4.14 Global-Audience Prediction

our global-audience prediction is verified by our dataset. In Fig. 4.14a, each sample is a content's current popularity versus its popularity in the previous timeslot. We observe that the assumption that a video has a global audience is highly violating over time, with a very small correlation between the current audience number and previous number. Our prediction is illustrated in Fig. 4.14b. Each sample represents the current popularity versus the global-audience index of the previous timeslot. We observe that after incorporating the propagation patterns, the correlation coefficient is increased by a factor of 4, thus indicating that the popularity can be better predicted by our design.

4.5.1.3   Local-Audience Prediction

In our architecture, a peer locally performs the cache replacement using not only the perceived video popularity but also the local social factors. To determine which videos should be kept for peering neighbors, we design a local-audience predictor based on the following information at peer i: (1) the local popularity which is the number of requests for video v received by peer i, denoted as p_i^v; (2) the fraction of peer i's friends that can join the propagation tree of video v, denoted as f_i^v. f_i^v is calculated by historical records for different video categories, i.e., peer i keeps a record of the fraction of friends that have been attracted in each category in the history; and (3) the time lag between the time when propagation tree is constructed and the time when the peer re-shares the video, i.e., $\tau_v^{(T)}$. Based on the social propagation patterns, we design a local-audience index to perform the prediction as follows:

$$q_v = z_s(\tau_v^{(T)})(p_i^v f_i^v).$$

In the peer-assisted replication, videos with a smaller local-audience index are more likely to be dumped by the peer. The rationale is that larger $p_i^v f_i^v$ indicates that

Fig. 4.15 Number of
regions in the propagation
versus the size of the
propagation

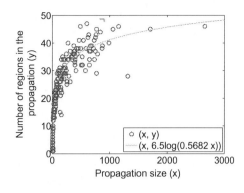

Fig. 4.16 CDF of
preference of local friends

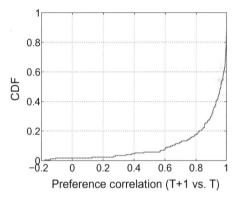

peer i can potentially attract more users to re-share video v from its friends in the
future, and $\tau_v^{(T)}$ is utilized to reflect the temporal locality.

The effectiveness of the local-audience predictor is also verified by our data.
Figure 4.16 illustrates the CDF of the correlation coefficient between a friend's video
category preference (calculated as a category preference vector) at time T and the
category preference at time $T-1$. We observe that most of the friends' preference can
be inferred from their historical preference. In our dataset, the correlation coefficient
for 80% of the user preference in two consecutive timeslots can be greater than 0.8.

4.5.2   Replication Strategies Based on Propagation Prediction

4.5.2.1   Region Selection in Edge-Cloud Replication

Based on the region prediction and the global-audience prediction, we first select the
videos to be replicated and determine regions they should be replicated to; then, we
reserve upload bandwidth at edge-cloud servers for them. When performing video
replication, we need to identify the videos that may propagate to more regions in

the future. We use the geographic influence index in the region prediction for this purpose. To achieve a better video download quality, a video with a greater $g_v^{(T)}$ should be replicated to more regions to serve users locally. The parameters c_1 and c_2 are selected according to the measurement. Based on the geographic influence index, we can predict whether the regions where the video has been replicated are sufficient.

Initial Replication. After video v is first generated by a user in the online social network, it will be stored by a server that is closest to the user's friends. Let $d_{r,i}, i \in \mathscr{F}_v$ denote the geographic distance between region r and user i, where $\mathscr{F}_v$ is the set of friends of the root user of video v (a "distance" based on Internet connectivity measurement can also be used, e.g., bandwidth or RTT). The initial region is then selected by solving the following problem: $r_v = \arg\min_{r \in \mathscr{R}} \sum_{i \in \mathscr{F}_v} d_{r,i}$, where $\mathscr{R}$ is the set of regions that can be used for the replication (determined by the cloud providers) and r_v is the region selected for the replication.

Selecting Existing Videos for Replication. According to our measurement study, we observe that although there are a massive number of videos in the online social network, in each timeslot, only limited videos are shared among users. In particular, we observe that among the 350,860 videos that we study in our measurement, only 1919 of them are re-shared in one timeslot (1 h) on average. Thus, in each timeslot, only a little fraction of existing videos need to be replicated to improve the service quality. How should we select the candidate videos for replication? We observe that the overlapping fraction of the common videos that are re-shared in timeslot T and $T - 1$ over all videos re-shared in timeslot T can be as large as 49%. In our design, the replication video set $\mathscr{V}^{(T)}$ is constructed as follows. (1) We build a candidate video set $\mathscr{W}^{(T)}$ by selecting videos that are imported or re-shared in the previous timeslot. In particular, we randomly choose 80% of the videos that have been imported or re-shared in the previous timeslot and 20% of the videos among the most popular ones in history. (2) We choose the videos in $\mathscr{W}^{(T)}$ that have the geographic influence index $g_v^{(T)}$ greater than $\theta_v^{(T+1)}$, which is a control parameter depending on the current replication status of video v, to form the video replication set $\mathscr{V}^{(T)}$. In our experiments, we let $\theta_v^{(T)} = 0.8|\mathscr{R}_v^{(T)}|$, where $\mathscr{R}_v^{(T)}$ is the set of regions that v has been replicated to. The rationale is that a video should be replicated to more regions if its current replication is under the requirement estimated from the geographic influence index.

Selecting Replication Regions for Videos in $\mathscr{V}^{(T)}$. After $\mathscr{V}^{(T)}$ has been constructed, the videos in $\mathscr{V}^{(T)}$ need to be replicated to more regions. Since these videos are the candidates that can attract users from more regions, we have to determine which videos need to be replicated to which regions. In our design, we extend the replication of a video to one more region each time. The selection of the region is similar to the approach used in the initial region selection. We minimize the geographic distance between the region and the potential users who may join the propagation tree. Let $\mathscr{L}_v^{(T)}$ denote the set of users who join the propagation tree in the previous timeslot. The selection is as follows:

$$r_v = \arg \min_{r \in \mathscr{R} - \mathscr{R}_v^{(T)}} \sum_{i \in \bigcup_{k \in \mathscr{L}_v^{(T)}} \mathscr{F}_k} d_{r,i},$$

where $\mathscr{F}_k$ is the friend set of user k. The rationale is that users in $\mathscr{L}_v^{(T)}$ are the ones who join the propagation tree in the previous timeslot, and it is likely for them to attract new users of the video, due to the temporal locality of the propagation. We utilize these users' friends' locations as a sample of all the users that can join the propagation tree and select the region that is closest to all the users. The benefit of always extending a video to a new region in the replication (i.e., r_v is selected from $\mathscr{R} - \mathscr{R}_v^{(T)}$) is that users in a popular propagation tree can choose more regions to download the video content from, and our scheme improves the possibility for them to select their preferred regions.

4.5.2.2 Bandwidth Reservation for Social Content at Edge-Cloud Servers

In each schedule round, we need to allocate upload bandwidths at the edge-cloud servers for the videos replicated. In our design, the bandwidth reservation depends on the social propagation strength, which can be evaluated using the global-audience index $e_v^{(T)}$. Let $\mathscr{V}_r$ denote the set of videos that are replicated in region r, the bandwidth reservation is then performed as follows:

$$b_{v,r_v} = B_{r_v} e_v^{(T)} / \sum_{v \in \mathscr{V}_{r_v}} e_v^{(T)}, \forall v \in \mathscr{V}^{(T)},$$

where b_{v,r_v} is the amount of bandwidth to be reserved for video v in the selected replication region r_v when the region is fully loaded with requests; and a video can extend to use more than b_{v,r_v} when the region is not fully loaded. B_r is the upload capacity of region r. The rationale of the bandwidth reservation is that videos with larger $e_v^{(T)}$ tend to attract more users in the propagation in the near future, and more upload bandwidth should be allocated for these videos' propagation to benefit the potential downloaders. Our edge-cloud replication algorithm is illustrated in Algorithm 6.

4.5.2.3 Cache Replacement in Peer-Assisted Replication

In Sect. 4.4, we have justified that the unique propagation pattern makes it very promising to utilized the peer-assisted paradigm to allocate certain amount of resource from the users to replicate the video content, and peers (users) can serve their social neighbors with good Internet connectivity. In our peer-assisted replication, we assume that users download video content according to their own demands, and we design a socially aware cache replacement strategy for peers to determine

---

Algorithm 6 Edge-Cloud Replication Algorithm.

1: **procedure** VIDEO AND REGION SELECTION
2:     $\mathscr{V}^{(T)} \leftarrow \Phi$
3:     **if** v is newly published **then**
4:         $\mathscr{V}^{(T)} \leftarrow \mathscr{V}^{(T)} \cup \{v\}$
5:         $r_v \leftarrow \arg\min_{r \in \mathscr{R}} \sum_{i \in \mathscr{F}_v} d_{r,i}$
6:     **else**
7:         **if** $v \in \mathscr{W}^{(T)}$ **and** $g_v^{(T)} > \theta_v^{(T+1)}$ **then**
8:             $\mathscr{V}^{(T)} \leftarrow \mathscr{V}^{(T)} \cup \{v\}$
9:             $r_v \leftarrow \arg\min_{r \in \mathscr{R} - \mathscr{R}_v^{(T)}} \sum_{i \in \bigcup_{k \in \mathscr{L}_v^{(T)}} \mathscr{F}_k} d_{r,i}$
10:       **end if**
11:    **end if**
12: **end procedure**
13: **procedure** BANDWIDTH RESERVATION
14:     **for all** $v \in \mathscr{V}^{(T)}$ **do**
15:         **if** v is replicated at region r_v **then**
16:             $b_{v,r_v} \leftarrow B_{r_v} e_v^{(T)} / \sum_{v \in \mathscr{V}_{r_v}} e_v^{(T)}$
17:         **end if**
18:     **end for**
19: **end procedure**

---

which videos are cached to help other users, since peers' cache strategy can greatly affect the performance of a P2P system [19].

Peer Cache Replacement. Large local-audience index indicates that the video can be potentially downloaded by more local friends, and the peer should keep it to serve these friends. Thus, in our cache replacement algorithm, the peer will try to dump videos with the smallest q_v's until the capacity is enough for new videos. In Sect. 4.6, we will present the effectiveness of our cache replacement for social content.

4.6 Performance Evaluation

In this section, we conduct experiments using traces from Tencent Weibo to verify our design and evaluate its performance.

4.6.1 Experiment Setup

Based on the same traces used in our measurement, we randomly select 9,318 videos from the original traces in the last 10 days for our experiments. These videos propagate among the regions captured by Tencent Weibo—the propagation traces are used for video replication using our design. The length of a timeslot is set to 1 h, as used in our measurement studied. Peers are located in the regions according to their profiles, and an edge-cloud server is deployed in each region. In our

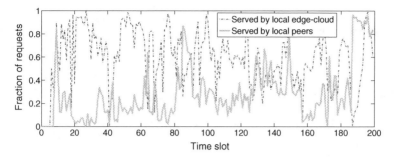

Fig. 4.17 Servers

experiments, we assume that the records of imports and re-shares indicate users' downloads of these videos. Thus, these records are used to drive users' downloads in the simulation. We also assume the user-generated videos have the same short duration [6], and we let the replication unit be a whole video for both servers and peers. We normalize the geographic distance between peers and servers in the evaluation. In the peer-assisted replication, peers exchange their cache states with socially connected neighbors periodically, such that they are aware of what can be downloaded from these social neighbors. When downloading from other peers, a tracker server is employed to help peers find each other. A peer downloads a video according to the following rules: (1) it first tries to download the video from neighboring peers, where peers that are socially connected in the same region are prioritized; (2) if no peer is able to serve the video, it will resort to the edge-cloud servers in the same region; and (3) if the local servers are not able to serve it, it will try other servers with the smallest geographic distances.

We first show the performance of PSAR over time. Figure 4.17 illustrates the fraction of requests served by their local edge-cloud servers over all server-served requests and the fraction of requests served by local peers over all peer-served requests. We observe that our replication can reach relatively high levels of requests that are served by local edge-cloud servers and local peers (58.7% and 28.5%, respectively). Meanwhile, in PSAR, we observe that the local edge-cloud servers and peers can compensate each other to serve the users over time. Next, we will evaluate the detailed performance of PSAR.

4.6.2   Efficiency of Edge-Cloud Replication

In the edge-cloud replication, we compare PSAR with the following algorithms that are widely used in real-world video service systems. (1) A popularity-based replication, where videos are prioritized to be replicated or removed according to the videos' historical popularity, i.e., the number of total imports and re-shares in a recent period. The videos selected for replication are assigned to regions such that

Fig. 4.18 Local download
ratio versus server capacity

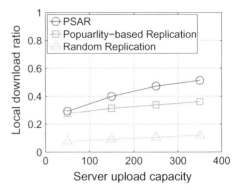

the load (overall popularity of videos) can be balanced among the regions. In each
region, the edge-cloud server allocates upload bandwidth for a video proportionally
to its recent popularity. (2) A random approach where videos are replicated randomly
in different regions and reserved with a random amount of upload bandwidth. Note
that these two algorithms are also executed periodically in each timeslot.

Fraction of Locally Served Requests. We first evaluate how many requests of
videos can be served by local servers using different replication algorithms. We
define a local download ratio as the fraction of requests that are served by users'
local servers, i.e., servers in the same geographic region with the users issuing the
requests. Figure 4.18 illustrates the local download ratio versus the average upload
capacity allocated at an edge-cloud server. We observe that our edge-cloud replication
in PSAR can improve the local download ratio by more than 30% compared with the
popularity-based scheme, and as the available server bandwidth capacity grows, the
local download ratio in PSAR increases faster than the popularity-based and random
algorithms, thus indicating that users can benefit more from the increased server
resource in PSAR.

Normalized Download Geo-Distance from Servers. We also evaluate the normalized download distance, which is defined as the average normalized geographic
distance between the users and the servers from which they download the videos.
Figure 4.19 illustrates the normalized download distance versus the average server

Fig. 4.19 Normalized
download distance versus
server capacity

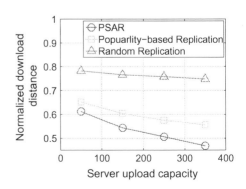

capacity. We observe that PSAR achieves a smaller download distance than the other two algorithms. The reason is that by inferring the geographic influence index, the global-audience index and users' social connections, better prediction of a video's propagation range can be utilized to perform the region selection. Similarly, we observe that the normalized download distance in PSAR decreases faster than other algorithms when the server capacity increases.

Number of Replications. We further study the impact of the number of replications of a video on the service quality. Figure 4.20 compares the local download ratio of a video in the three strategies in terms of different numbers of video replications. We observe that in the random replication, all the videos have the similar number of replications—this is the reason for its inefficiency for contents that are either very popular or only shared among small social groups. The replication number in the popularity-based replication is similar to that in PSAR; however, PSAR is more effective when replicating videos that are shared in small social groups and the ones that are highly propagating across many regions—more than 4 times the number of unpopular requests can be served by local servers or peers.

Fig. 4.20 Local download ratio of a video versus the number of its replications

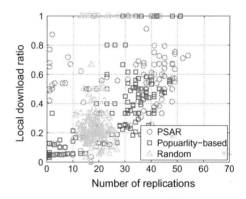

Fig. 4.21 Peer contribution versus the number of social hops between the pair of peers

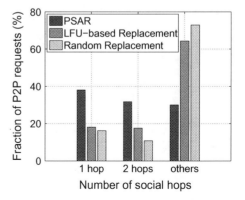

4.6.3 Efficiency of Peer-Assisted Replication

We also evaluate the efficiency of the peer-assisted replication. We compare PSAR with (1) an LFU-based peer cache replacement algorithm, in which the videos least requested recently (a reference time window of 24 h) are dumped to make room for new ones, (2) an LRU-based cache replacement algorithm, in which videos that have not been recently requested are dumped, and (3) a random replacement algorithm, in which randomly selected videos are dumped.

Local Cache Hit Ratio. We first evaluate the local cache hit ratio, which is defined as the fraction of videos that can be directly downloaded from socially connected peers. A higher local cache hit ratio indicates better local download performance, since we have already justified that peers which are socially connected to each other are also geographically close to each other, thus resulting in a better Internet connectivity. Figure 4.22 illustrates the local cache hit ratio versus the storage capacity of each peer (the number of videos that can be stored). We observe that our design significantly improves the local cache hit ratio by more than 40% compared with the LRU and LFU schemes. Moreover, as the cache capacity increases, the cache hit ratio in our design improves much faster than in the other algorithms. The reason for the inefficiency of LFU and LRU is that many unpopular videos cannot be efficiently cached according to users' historical requests, whereas they can be addressed in our design where peers actively cache them for their friends based on the local-audience index. We also observe that LFU and LRU achieve similar ratios.

Normalized Download Geo-Distance from Peers. We also evaluate the normalized geographic distance between neighboring peers. Figure 4.23 illustrates the average normalized download distance between peers who upload videos to each other versus the cache storage capacity at each peer. We observe that our socially aware cache replacement achieves a much smaller geographic download distance than the other algorithms, which means that a peer is more likely to find a close neighbor to download the videos from, thereby achieving a better Internet connectivity for both sides. We also observe that when a large cache capacity is allocated at a peer, our design benefits more than other algorithms.

Fig. 4.22 Local cache hit ratio versus peer's capacity

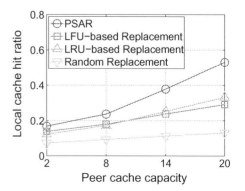

Fig. 4.23 Normalized
download distance versus
peer's capacity

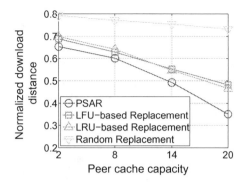

Socially Aware Contribution. We further investigate the P2P networks by studying which type of peers upload contents to the users. Figure 4.21 illustrates the fraction of requests served by peers versus the number of social hops between the pair of peers. We observe that in our design, more than 2 times the number of requests are served by their direct friends or two-hop friends in the social network, so that more local peers can be used to upload the content. The reason is that in PSAR, videos are cached according to not only the requests of users, but also the level of friends that can be influenced by the video in the future.

4.7   Discussion

In this section, we discuss the reduction of replications of social content, the collaboration of edge-cloud and peers, how our design can be effectively implemented, and the potential use of content information to aid the content replication.

Reduction of Replications. In our measurement study, we have shown the temporal locality of the social video propagation, i.e., after a period of time since its publication, a video content will not be able to attract as many users as before. Although the bandwidth reservation can adapt to reduce the upload capacity allocated for a video that becomes less popular, the replications of the video still occupy the storage at edge-cloud servers. Thus, we need to reduce a video's replications on the edge-cloud servers to make room for new videos generated by users in the system. Intuitive strategies for video reduction can be designed as follows: (1) the region where a video is mostly accessed can be selected as a permanent backup of the video; and (2) other regions where the video is replicated can locally dump the video contents according to their geographic influence index, i.e., videos with a smaller geographic influence index are more likely to be removed from an edge-cloud server to make room for new ones.

Collaboration between Edge-Cloud Servers and Peers. In the distribution of social video contents, edge-cloud servers and peers both serve the video download requests. The collaboration between them in PSAR is as follows: (1) the edge-cloud is mainly used to serve users with their preferred servers, and peers only assist in the unpopular videos; (2) in the online social network, friends are incentivized to upload content to each other, i.e., the social preference [11]; and (3) according to our design, peers are usually located close to each other. Because the cloud providers are deploying edge-cloud servers increasingly closer to users, it is a trend that peer distribution may only occur when users very close to each other, where energy-saving transfer approaches can be used.

Real-World Implementation. Propagation-based socially aware delivery of social content is a design incorporating both the content delivery system and the online social network. We discuss how the design can be implemented in a real system. (1) Data aspect (how social propagation is collected and mined). APIs are opened by the online social networks for third-parties to retrieve not only how content propagates between users but also how users are socially connected to each other. Moreover, they also provide mining and learning systems for data processing (e.g., Google Dremel)—a video distribution system can make use of such propagation information. (2) Delivery aspect (cloud-based and peer-assisted distribution). On the one hand, cloud providers such as Amazon have provided interfaces for the video service providers to elastically, dynamically and geographically allocate the cloud servers; on the other hand, content providers generally deploy clients (e.g., Apps for mobile devices), which enable peer-assisted delivery.

Content information. In our peer-assisted delivery method, the video category is used for friend preference mining. More content details of videos can still be explored, e.g., videos uploaded for sharing are often accompanied by metadata that describe the content, which can be leveraged to better aid the preference inference [20].

References

1. V.K. Adhikari, S. Jain, Z.L. Zhang, Where do you tube? uncovering youtube server selection strategy, in *IEEE International Conference on Computer Communications and Networks* (2011)
2. V.K. Adhikari et al., Reverse engineering the youtube video delivery cloud, in *IEEE Hot Topics in Media Delivery Workshop* (2011)
3. M. Arlitt, B. Krishnamurthy, P. Gill, A few chirps about twitter, in *ACM Workshop on Online Social Networks (WOSN)* (2008)
4. F. Benevenuto et al., Characterizing user behavior in online social networks, in *ACM Internet Measurement Conference (IMC)* (2009)
5. M. Cha, A. Mislove, K.P. Gummadi, A measurement driven analysis of information propagation in the Flickr social network, in *ACM International Conference on World Wide Web (WWW)* (2009)
6. X. Cheng, C. Dale, J. Liu, Statistics and social network of youtube videos, in *IEEE International Workshop on Quality of Service (IWQoS)* (2008)
7. X. Cheng, J. Liu, Load-balanced migration of social media to content clouds, in *ACM Network and Operating System Support for Digital Audio and Video (NOSSDAV)* (2011)
8. X. Cheng, J. Liu, NetTube: exploring social networks for peer-to- peer short video sharing, in *IEEE International Conference on Distributed Computing Systems (INFOCOM)* (2009)
9. P.S. Dodds, D.J. Watts, A generalized model of social and biological contagion. J. Theor. Biol. **232**(4), 587–604 (2005)

10. P. Domingos, M. Richardson, Mining the network value of customers, in *ACM SIGKDD Conference on Knowledge Discovery and Data Mining (KDD)* (2001)
11. E. Fehr, U. Fischbacher, Why social preferences matter-the impact of non-selfish motives on competition, cooperation and incentives. Econ. J. **112**(478), C1–C33 (2002)
12. J. Hartline, V. Mirrokni, M. Sundararajan, Optimal marketing strategies over social networks, in *ACM International Conference on World Wide Web (WWW)* (2008)
13. B. Huffaker et al., Distance metrics in the internet, in *IEEE International Telecommunications Symposium* (2002)
14. J. Kangasharju, J. Roberts, K.W. Ross, Object replication strategies in content distribution networks. Comput. Commun. **25**(4), 376–383 (2002)
15. D. Kempe, J. Kleinberg, E. Tardos, Maximizing the spread of influence through a social network, in *ACM SIGKDD Conference on Knowledge Discovery and Data Mining (KDD)* (2003)
16. H. Kwak et al., What is twitter, a social network or a news media?, in *ACM International Conference on World Wide Web (WWW)* (2010)
17. H. Li, H. Wang, J. Liu, Video sharing in online social network: measurement and analysis, in *ACM Network and Operating System Support for Digital Audio and Video (NOSSDAV)* (2012)
18. Y. Liu, Y. Guo, C. Liang, A survey on peer-to-peer video streaming systems. Peer-to-Per Netw. Appl. **1**(1), 18–28 (2008)
19. J.G. Luo et al., A trace-driven approach to evaluate the scalability of p2pbased video-on-demand service. IEEE Trans. Parallel Distrib. Syst. (TPDS) **20**(1), 59–70 (2009)
20. P. Melville, R.J. Mooney, R. Nagarajan, Content-boosted collaborative filtering for improved recommendations, in *The National Conference on Artificial Intelligence* (2002)
21. A. Mislove, RethinkingWeb content distribution in the social media era, in *NSF Workshop on Social Networks and Mobility in the Cloud* (2012). 4.7 Discussion 79
22. A. Mislove et al., Measurement and analysis of online social networks, in *ACM Internet Measurement Conference (IMC)* (2007)
23. A. Mislove et al., You are who you know: inferring user profiles in online social networks, in *ACM International Conference on Web Search and Data Mining (WSDM)* (2010)
24. K. Nguyen et al., Preserving social locality in data replication for social networks, in *IEEE International Conference on Distributed Computing Systems (ICDCS) Workshop on Simplifying Complex Networks for Practitioners* (2011)
25. G. Peng, CDN: content distribution network, in *arXiv preprint cs/0411069* (2004)
26. J.M. Pujol et al., The little engine(s) that could: scaling online social networks. SIGCOMM Comput. Commun. Rev. **40**, 375–386 (2010). ISSN: 0146-4833. http://doi.acm.org/10.1145/1851275.1851227
27. S. Scellato et al., Distance matters: geo-social metrics for online social networks, in *USENIX Conference on Online social networks* (2010)
28. D.A. Tran, K. Nguyen, C. Pham, S-CLONE: socially-aware data replication for social networks. Comput. Netw. 56.7, 2001–2013 (2012). ISSN: 1389-1286. https://doi.org/10.1016/j.comnet.2012.02.010. http://www.sciencedirect.com/science/article/pii/S1389128612000746
29. Z. Wang et al., Guiding internet-scale video service deployment using microblog-based prediction, in *IEEE International Conference on Distributed Computing Systems (INFOCOM)* (2012)
30. Z. Wang et al., Propagation-based social-aware replication for social video contents, in *ACM International Conference on Multimedia (Multimedia)* (2012)
31. Wiki: Clustering/Coefficient. http://en.wikipedia.org/wiki/Clusteringcoefficient (2013)
32. Y. Wu et al., Scaling social media applications into geo-distributed clouds, in *IEEE International Conference on Distributed Computing Systems (INFOCOM)* (2012)
33. D. Xu et al., Analysis of a CDN-P2P hybrid architecture for cost-effective streaming media distribution. Multimedia Syst. **11**(4), 383–399 (2006)
34. W. Zhu et al., Multimedia cloud computing. IEEE Signal Process. Mag. **28**(3), 59–69 (2011)

Chapter 5
Joint Online Processing and Geo-Distributed Delivery for Dynamic Social Streaming

Abstract To satisfy the dynamical demands from different social content consumers, it is promising to "customize" content according to users' unique demands. Such customization usually requires computation resources in the content delivery flow. This chapter presents some exploration into incorporating content processing in the social content delivery framework.

Keywords Content processing · Transcoding · Cloud-edge paradigm

5.1 Introduction

Dynamic adaptive streaming over HTTP (DASH) has emerged as a popular video streaming method [10], in which content providers can leverage the largely-deployed CDN servers to cache and deliver the video segments [4].[1] Adaptive streaming has been widely implemented and supported by the industry, including Apple HTTP Live Streaming, Microsoft Live Smooth Streaming, and Adobe Adaptive Streaming. It allows users with heterogeneous and dynamically changing network conditions to receive an adaptive bitrate, achieving the best video streaming experience in different contexts [15].

In adaptive streaming, video service providers have to not only deliver the video *segments* (data blocks in a video that can be downloaded over HTTP and played independently) but also transcode the videos to different *versions* (i.e., videos with different bitrates but the same content) for the users. In this chapter, we refer to *transcoding* as transcoding a video to different bitrates, which may consume significant computational resources [12]. To date, traditional approaches separately perform the video transcoding and delivery—being unaware of which segments users will request, they have to transcode every video published to a set of fixed versions and replicate segments of different versions using the same strategy.

Problems with the traditional approaches for adaptive streaming include the following: (1) prefixed versions only allow users to choose from a small set of candidate

---

[1] ©[2016] IEEE. Reprinted, with permission, from IEEE Transactions on Parallel and Distributed Systems.

© The Author(s) 2018
Z. Wang et al., *Online Social Media Content Delivery*,
SpringerBriefs in Computer Science, https://doi.org/10.1007/978-981-10-2774-1_5

bitrates, which cannot effectively adapt to the changing network conditions. (2) To address this problem, video providers increase the number of adaptive versions— as both the number of uploaded videos and the number of versions are increasing, a significant amount of computational resources are required to transcode all the videos to all the versions [11]. As the popularity distribution of video segments is becoming significantly heavy-tailed, i.e., a substantial fraction of video segments are not requested at all—pre-transcoding them could be a significant waste of valuable computational resources. The situation is exacerbated by today's user-generated-content (UGC)-based video sharing services [5]. (3) On the other hand, traditional approaches are not aware of the users' *preferences* for different *peering servers* (i.e., servers directly uploading the video segments to users) when users receive segments of different versions, leading to a mismatch between the download speed and the required segment bitrate, e.g., a user being able to receive a high-bitrate segment might be redirected to a peering server with a slow connection to the user [1].

To address these problems, we propose to jointly schedule segment transcoding and delivery in an online manner using geo-distributed computation and communication resources. The new design philosophy allows us to jointly optimize the streaming quality for users and minimize the computation and bandwidth cost for transcoding and replicating the video segments. To study the benefits of our proposal for real-world video providers, we measure the user request patterns of adaptive video streams in a representative video streaming service in China, BesTV [3] (an IPTV system serving over 16 million users). We have made the following observations: (i) due to the skewness of popularity distribution of the videos, segments and versions, the online transcoding paradigm has the potential to significantly reduce the computational resources required.

To demonstrate that our proposal can be implemented practically in today's CDNs which are already widely used for adaptive video streaming, we further measure the availability of computation and bandwidth resources in Tencent CDN [16], which serves more than 70% of the traffic from one of the largest content providers in China. We have further made the following observations: (i) a substantial amount of idle computational resources can be provided by the *backend servers* (i.e., servers supporting the peering servers), and the idle computational resources are relatively stable over time, thus indicating that online transcoding can be effectively performed by these backend servers. (ii) Since peering servers are deployed at different geographic locations with different Internet Service Providers (ISPs), and scheduled to serve different numbers of user requests, the distribution of users' download speeds differs across different CDN regions, i.e., (1) users have different preferences of CDN servers in different regions from which to receive segments, whereas (2) servers in different regions have different preferences of versions of video segments to transcode.

To the best of our knowledge, our study is the first to explore the new design space of joint online transcoding and geo-distributed delivery. Our contributions are summarized as follows: (1) we conduct large-scale measurement studies to motivate our approach, the feasibility of its implementation, and the guidelines for our design; (2) to achieve good streaming quality, low computational resource consumption, and low video segment replication cost, we connect video transcoding and video delivery based on users' region preferences and regional version preferences—we use users' preferences for regions to redirect them to their ideal peering servers, and we use the regional version preferences to schedule the transcoding tasks; (3) we formulate the problems, design practical algorithms to solve them, and demonstrate the performance of our design.

The rest of the chapter is organized as follows. We present the measurement insights that motivate our design in Sect. 5.3. We present our detailed design in Sect. 5.4. We verify the effectiveness and evaluate its performance in Sect. 5.5. We discuss related works in Sect. 5.2.

5.2 Related Work

Many architectures have been proposed to implement large-scale video streaming services, including the CDN-based architecture [14]. After HTTP became the norm for users to access online content, multimedia applications, including video streaming, have been largely deployed over HTTP. CDNs can significantly assist in HTTP-based streaming with servers deployed in multiple geographical locations across multiple ISPs [17]. Users experience higher-quality streaming by receiving streams at more reliable bandwidth from the CDN servers. Recently, Adhikari et al. [1] proposed a multi-CDN scheme for real-world video systems to further improve the streaming quality. Traditional studies regarding video streaming have focused on improving the connectivity between streaming servers and users from the network aspect.

Based on the CDN delivery backbone, DASH has recently been proposed to provide adaptive video streaming for heterogeneous networks and devices [10]. Compared with the traditional video streaming paradigm, DASH enables a much larger number of quality versions, requiring a significant amount of computational resources to transcode these versions of videos. Dedicated transcoders are developed to accelerate video transcoding [18]. There have also been works regarding using the computational resources in a cloud cluster for video transcoding. Lao et al. [11] designed a MapReduce-based video transcoding scheme for distributing transcoding tasks. Huang et al. [9] proposed CloudStream, which schedules the video transcoding tasks inside a cluster according to properties of the videos. Traditional studies regarding video transcoding have exploited dedicated devices or computational resources, leading to the decoupling of segment transcoding and delivery.

Most related works regarding adaptive streaming have investigated video delivery and video transcoding separately, i.e., videos are pre-transcoded centrally and then replicated to CDN servers for delivery using a same strategy, e.g., a full replication scheme. In this chapter, we explore the design space of joint transcoding and delivery using geo-distributed computation and network resources.

5.3   Measurements and Observations

We conduct measurement studies to motivate our design and summarize the derived design principles.

5.3.1   Measurement Setup

To demonstrate the benefits and feasibility of our proposal, we use large-scale measurement studies based on valuable traces collected from BesTV and Tencent CDN.

5.3.1.1   Traces of Users' Video Viewing Patterns

To study the potential of using an online transcoding scheme to save computational resources, we collected real-world traces of video access patterns in BesTV. In BesTV, videos are published in 17 categories and pre-transcoded into 4 versions (bitrates of 700, 1300, 2300 and 4000 Kbps). We collected the viewing activities of users in Heilongjiang province in November 2012 regarding how 190K videos were watched by users from over 3 million IP addresses. For each of the streaming sessions, the traces record which segments were downloaded by which users, including the time stamp when a segment was downloaded, the user ID, the video ID, the size and version of the segment, and the time spent downloading the segment. Using these traces, we demonstrate the great potential of our joint transcoding and streaming paradigm in Sect. 5.3.2.1.

5.3.1.2   Traces of CDN Characteristics

To study the feasibility of online transcoding in a CDN system, which has already been widely used for adaptive streaming [4], we collected traces of the backend and peering servers from Tencent CDN, as follows: (1) *CPU load patterns*. To study the computational resource availability for segment transcoding, we collected CPU load traces from the backend servers of Tencent CDN. In particular, the CPU load of 5,441 servers was recorded every 5 minutes for the whole month of March 2013. Each CPU load trace item contains the following information: timestamp and the CPU load recorded as the average number of processes waiting on each CPU core; a CPU load greater than 1 indicates that the server is fully loaded. (2) *Bandwidth patterns*. To study the users' preferences for CDN regions and the regional preferences of versions to transcode, we have collected traces including 3.39 billion TCP connections from peering servers located at 55 regions in May 2013. These TCP connections were established to download content with sizes varying from tens of bytes to 4.8 GB. Each of the trace items contains the following information: the timestamp indicating when a TCP connection was established, the client IP, the number of downloaded bytes and the connection duration. In Sect. 5.3.2.2, we use these traces to study the feasibility and provide guidelines for our design.

5.3.2 Measurement Insights

5.3.2.1 Potential—Computational Resources to Be Saved

Based on the video viewing records from BesTV, Fig. 5.1a illustrates the popularity distribution of the videos. Each sample represents the number of user requests of a video in one month versus the rank of the video. We observe that over 53% of these videos had no viewer in a month. This can be explained by the fact that in today's video sharing services, that the time users spend watching videos has grown much more slowly than the number of videos, and such skewness of the popularity distribution is also prevalent in other UGC-based video sharing systems, such as YouTube [5].

In Fig. 5.1a, only 13% of the videos have a monthly number of views greater than 500. We further investigate how different segments with different versions inside a relatively popular video (with approximately 1,000 segments) are requested by users. Figure 5.1b illustrates the distribution of the requests for segments of one of the most popular videos. Each curve represents the number of segment requests versus the segment index. We observe that (1) only a small range of segments are requested by many users, e.g., the first tens of the segments; (2) different versions receive different numbers of requests, e.g., the version with a bitrate of 4000 Kbps is requested by many more users; and (3) a large fraction of segments are requested by nobody for some versions, e.g., the last segments of the 700 and 1300 Kbps versions.

These observations indicate that as increasingly many videos are published, by both professional content providers and individuals, pre-transcoding every segment of all videos into an increasing number of versions can be a significant waste of computational resources; this waste motivates our segment-based online transcoding.

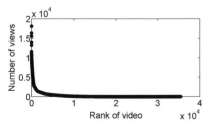
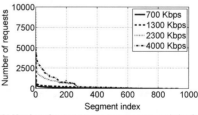

(a) Number of user views versus video rank.

(b) Number of segment requests versus segment index for different versions.

Fig. 5.1 Popularity of videos, segments and versions in BesTV (Heilongjiang, November 2012)

5.3.2.2 Possibility—Computational Resources Available in CDN

Inspired by Akamai's real-time monitoring [7] that the CPU load of CDN servers not only can be efficiently measured but is also diverse across different servers, we first demonstrate the availability of idle computational resources in the CDN. Figure 5.2a plots the CPU load—the average number of processes waiting on each CPU core of the backend servers in a time slot of 15 minutes. We observe that in a particular time slot, the CPU load of the 5,441 backend servers ivaries from around 0 to 8.6, and as many as 72.4% (resp. 55.9%) of backend servers have a CPU load smaller than 1.0 (resp. 0.5), thus indicating that a substantial amount of available computational resources in the CDN can be allocated for video transcoding. The reason for the high availability of the computational resources in a CDN is that many backend servers are only assigned simple I/O tasks, e.g., loading data from the distributed storage system for the peering servers.

We further study the availability of computational resources in a region of the CDN. We use a city-ISP pair to identify a region. Figure 5.2b illustrates the regional CPU load, i.e., the average CPU load of all the backend servers in that region. In this figure, each curve represents the CPU load of the four largest regions, i.e., Xian, Tianjin, Chengdu and Beijing, in one day. We also observe the existence of available computational resources at the regional level; moreover, we observe that the CPU load differs across different regions, e.g., the CPU load of Xian is much lower than that of Beijing on that day.

To utilize the idle CPU resource from the backend servers in the CDN for segment transcoding, we also need to investigate the stability of the idle computational resources on the backend servers. Since these servers can be scheduled to run different tasks, the available computational resources provided by these servers may vary over time. We use an average coefficient of variation to evaluate the daily churning level of the CPU load of a backend server, which is calculated as follows: $CV = 1/24 \sum_{h=0}^{23} \sqrt{E[(X_h - \bar{X}_h)^2]}/\bar{X}_h$, where X_h represents a set of CPU load records of a particular server in one hour h, i.e., there are 12 samples in an hour, as the CPU load is recorded every 5 minutes. A large CV implies a highly churning CPU load over time. In Fig. 5.3a, we sample 3 servers with different CV's on March

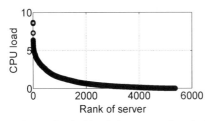
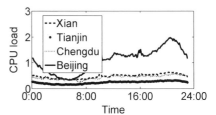

(a) Average CPU load in 15 minutes versus the rank of the server (8PM, March 5, 2013).

(b) Average CPU load on servers in different regions over time (March 5, 2013).

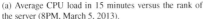

Fig. 5.2 Average CPU load of backend servers

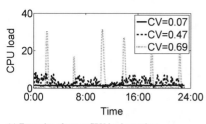
(a) Examples of server CPU load over time.

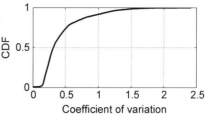
(b) The CDF of the coefficient of variation of the server CPU load.

Fig. 5.3 Variation in the server CPU load over time

5, 2013. Each curve represents the CPU load of the server over time. We observe that servers with $CV = 0.07$ and $CV = 0.47$ have a stable CPU load over time, whereas the server with $CV = 0.69$ has a relatively churning CPU load, varying from 0.17 to 31.5 in several minutes.

We investigate the distribution of CVs of all the backend servers in the CDN. In Fig. 5.3b, the curve represents the CDF of CVs of all the servers on the same day. We observe that more than 70% of the servers have a CV smaller than 0.5, thus indicating that the CPU load of many backend servers is relatively stable—their capacity for performing video transcoding in the near future can be predicted. We use such information in our design of transcoding task scheduling.

5.3.2.3 Connections—Users' Region Preferences and Regional Version Preferences

In the context of online transcoding, we are allowed the degree of freedom that segments can be transcoded by different CDN regions. Next, we explore the guidelines for such transcoding schedule.

- *Users' preferences of different CDN regions.* Which version of a video segment is requested by a user depends on the user's download speed. Based on the TCP traces of the peering servers, we compare the download speed of about 150 users who downloaded from different peering servers in the same 10 minutes on May 4, 2013. In Fig. 5.4, each sample is the average download speed of a user downloading from a peering server deployed in Shanghai versus the average download speed of the same user downloading from a Shenzhen peering server, both with the same ISP. We observe that for more than 79% of the users, their download speeds differ by more than a factor of 2 when they download from servers located in different regions, thus indicating that redirecting users to their ideal peering servers can help users receive a better streaming quality.
- *Regional preferences of different versions to transcode.* On the other hand, to study the regional preference of versions to transcode, we calculate the average download speeds of users downloading from the peering servers. In Fig. 5.5, each

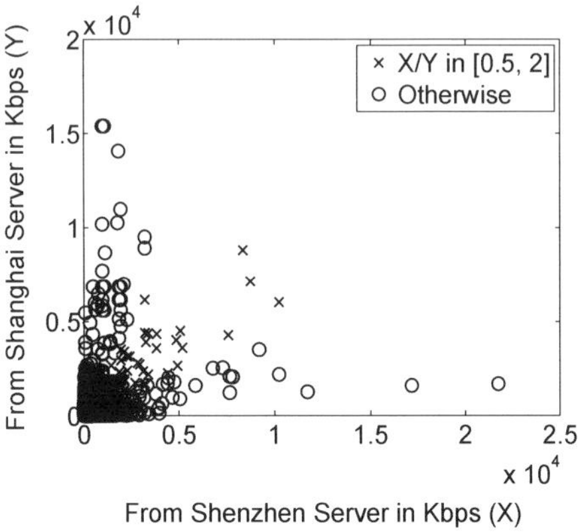

Fig. 5.4 Comparison of average download speed of users downloading from different peering servers in the same 10 minutes on May 4, 2013

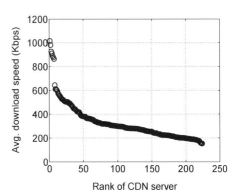

Fig. 5.5 Average user download speed of different peering servers on May 4, 2013

sample represents the average download speed in one day, of all users served by a server versus the rank of the server. We observe that the average download speed varies quite significantly across these peering servers, from 170 to 1.1 Mbps.

We further study the download speeds from servers in different regions, i.e., the download speeds from servers in different regions to users. In Fig. 5.6, each bar represents the minimum, average and maximum download speeds from the peering servers in a region. We observe that the average download speeds across different regions vary from 180 Kbps (region BJT, i.e., Beijing, China Telecom) to 512 Kbps (region ZJM, i.e., Zhejiang, China Mobile). Different regions "cover" users with quite different speeds, e.g., BJT serves most of the low-bitrate users, whereas ZJM serves hit-bitrate users. The rationale behind these observations is as follows: (1) peering servers are physically deployed at different locations and with different ISPs, such that the Internet connectivity and average bandwidth capacity are different, and (2) peering servers at different regions are generally scheduled to serve different numbers of user requests, thus leading to the different server load.

These observations indicate that servers in different regions have different preferences of versions to transcode, e.g., a region with a low CDN-to-user download

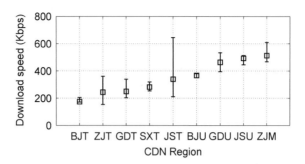

Fig. 5.6 Average user download speed in different CDN regions on May 4, 2013

speed may prefer to produce low-bitrate segments. Satisfying such preferences of regions can reduce the *cost* of replicating transcoded segments, since segments are already transcoded where they are requested.

5.4   Joint Online Transcoding and Geo-Distributed Delivery

5.4.1   Framework

Figure 5.7 illustrates our design, where segments in different versions of videos are transcoded upon users' requests. In this example, $s1, s2, s3, s4$ represent segments of different versions, which are requested by a user during her streaming session. $R1, R2$ and $R3$ are CDN *regions* (each is represented by a pair of a geographical location and ISP) where servers are deployed with backend servers and peering servers deployed. Segments can be transcoded by selected regions (e.g., $s2$ is transcoded by region $R1$), replicated between regions (e.g., $s1$ is replicated from region $R3$ to $R1$), and delivered to users, all in an online manner.

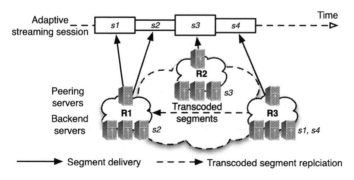

Fig. 5.7 Joint online transcoding and geo-distributed streaming: an illustration

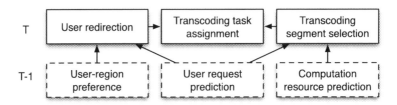

Fig. 5.8 Framework of our joint online transcoding and delivery mechanism

Figure 5.8 further illustrates the framework of our online transcoding and delivery scheme, which schedules segment transcoding and replication periodically: based on the recent information collected in time slot $T - 1$, we perform transcoding and replication of segments that are likely to be requested in time slot T. The collected information include the following: (1) users' preferences of different regions to receive segments. In our design, we allow users to use a bandwidth estimation approach (e.g., abget [2]m which uses little bandwidth to measure the end-to-end bandwidth) to rank a set of candidate peering servers, in the descending order of the estimated download speed. (2) The number of requests for a particular segment, which can be predicted according to users' segment requests in previous time slots. Based on the estimation of CDN-to-user bandwidth and users' segment requests, we are able to estimate which segments will be requested by users in the next time slot and the request level of each segment. (3) The idle computational resources. Because many backend servers have stable CPU loads over time according to our measurement study, we use the level of computational resources in the current time slot as the available computational resources in the next time slot. Other regression models (e.g., ARIMA [19]) can also be explored to achieve better prediction accuracy, which we will investigate in the future.

Using such information, we perform the following: (1) *user redirection*. To enable high-quality streaming, our design redirects users to their ideal regions such that they can receive segments at high bitrates. We redirect users at a region level, i.e., the region with the highest CDN-to-user bandwidth is selected serve a user's request, and peering servers in the same region are assigned to serve user requests in a round-robin manner. (2) *Transcoding segment selection*. Backend servers with idle CPU resources perform video transcoding by slicing a video into multiple closed groups of pictures (GoPs), each of which can be transcoded independently [9]. To enable smooth playback, when a segment request of a particular version is not transcoded in a timely manner, we send the user the segment of an alternative version, whose bitrate is closest to that of the requested version. We prioritize more "important" segments that are more critical to users' streaming quality to be transcoded when computational resources are insufficient. (3) *Transcoding task assignment*. A transcoded segment is cached by the backend servers and replicated to other regions, according to our replication strategy. Transcoding is performed by strategically selected regions such that the cost of replicating the transcoded segments to other regions can be minimized.

Before we present the design details, Table 5.1 presents important notation used in this chapter.

Table 5.1 Notations for joint online processing and delivery

Symbol	Definition
$\mathbf{U}^{(T)}$	Set of users requesting segments in time slot T
$D^{(T)}(u, r)$	Binary variable indicating whether user u will download from region r in time slot T
$H(u, r)$	Preference level for user u to receive video stream from region r
W_r	Bandwidth capacity of region r
$e_{(s,v)}^{(T)}$	Importance level of a particular segment (s, v) in time slot T
$Q_{(s,v)}^{(T)}$	Number of requests of segment (s, v) from all regions in time slot T
$Y_{(s,v)}^{(T)}$	Quality gain if segment (s, v) is transcoded in time slot T
$B(v)$	Bitrate of a particular version v
$\mathbf{G}^{(T)}(s)$	The set of transcoded versions of segment s
$\mathbf{R}$	Set of CDN regions
$\mathbf{E}^{(T)}$	Set of segments to be transcoded in time slot T
$L(u, r)$	Highest version that u can receive when she downloads from region r
$C(s, v)$	computational resources required to perform the transcoding task to generate a segment s of version v
$I^{(T)}(r)$	Available computational resources that can be allocated for video transcoding from region r in time slot T
$F[(s, v), r]$	Overall replication cost when segment (s, v) is transcoded in region r
$A_{(s,v)}^{(T)}$	Region assigned to transcode segment (s, v) in time slot T

5.4.2   Quality-Driven Redirection

In our design, taking the advantage of online transcoding, a user can be redirected to her ideal region where segments are generated on the fly. This design principle allows users to choose a CDN region with the largest download speed to receive the segments, without considering the segment availability.

We first formulate this problem in a centralized manner. We denote $\mathbf{U}^{(T)}$ as the predicted set of users requesting different segments in the system in time slot T, and $\mathbf{R}$ as the set of CDN regions where a user can be redirected. We use $D^{(T)}$ to denote a redirection strategy, where the binary variable $D^{(T)}(u, r) = 1$ (resp. 0) indicates that user u will (resp. will not) be downloading from region r in the next time slot T.

In the context of adaptive video streaming, we assume that users expect to receive a large bitrate for good streaming quality whenever possible. Thus, we use $H(u, r)$ to denote user u's preference to download from a CDN region r. $H(u, r)$ can be defined as a concave increasing function of the estimated download speed achieved when user u downloads from peering servers in region r. We formulate the region-level user redirection as an optimization problem, as follows:

$$\max_{D^{(T)}} \sum_{u \in \mathbf{U}^{(T)}, r \in \mathbf{R}} H(u, r) D^{(T)}(u, r), \tag{5.1}$$

subject to:

$$\sum_{r \in \mathbf{R}} D^{(T)}(u, r) \leq 1, \forall u \in \mathbf{U}^{(T)},$$

$$\sum_{u \in \mathbf{U}^{(T)}} D^{(T)}(u, r) B(L(u, r)) \leq W_r, \forall r \in \mathbf{R},$$

where $B(v)$ is the bitrate of version v, $L(u, r)$ is the version with the highest bitrate that u can receive when she downloads from region r, and W_r is the bandwidth capacity of CDN region r. The rationale of the optimization is to maximize the streaming quality for users by the redirection.

This problem is generally NP-hard, since we can reduce a conventional 0–1 knapsack problem, which is NP-hard, to it. We design an algorithm to heuristically solve it in a distributed manner: (1) when a user starts to watch a video, the system assigns her a list of candidate peering servers from regions with the lowest load. (2) The user ranks these servers in descending order of the estimated download speeds as discussed in Sect. 5.4.1 and sends connection requests to these servers. (3) On the other hand, a peering server may receive connection requests from many users, and can only accept a limited number of users according to its available bandwidth W_r. User u is prioritized to be accepted if she has a larger $H(u, r)/B(L(u, r))$ with the CDN region r—this value reflects a marginal "gain" in streaming quality by a unit of bandwidth allocated. (4) The user selects the best peering server from the ones accepting her request according to the ranked list. In a real system, this algorithm can be effectively implemented and executed in a distributed manner.

5.4.3   Region-Preference-Aware Transcoding Schedule

After users are redirected to the CDN regions, they send requests for video segments of different versions. Based on the segment request prediction, we perform the transcoding task schedule, which proceeds in two steps: (1) we prioritize the segment transcoding tasks such that important segments are transcoded more urgently; (2) we distribute the transcoding tasks to CDN regions such that segments are transcoded where they are more likely to be requested.

5.4.3.1   Prioritizing Segment Transcoding Tasks

We prioritize the segment transcoding tasks according to the importance of these segments. We denote $e_{(s,v)}^{(T)}$ as the importance level of segment s of version v in time slot T. $e_{(s,v)}^{(T)}$ depends on the following factors: (1) the estimated number of user requests for the segment, which is discussed in Sect. 5.4.1, and (2) the quality-wise importance of the segment, which depends on the existing versions of the same segment. In particular, $e_{(s,v)}^{(T)}$ can be calculated as follows:

$$e_{(s,v)}^{(T)} = Q_{(s,v)}^{(T)} Y_{(s,v)}^{(T)},$$

where $Q_{(s,v)}^{(T)}$ denotes the predicted number of requests of the particular segment (s, v) in the next time slot T, and $Y_{(s,v)}^{(T)}$ is the quality gain if the segment is transcoded to version v. Figure 5.9 illustrates an example of the importance of a segment: a solid block represents a segment transcoded, and a dashed block represents one that is not transcoded yet. When segment $(s1, v3)$ and $(s2, v3)$ are both requested by the same number of users, $(s1, v3)$ is prioritized to be transcoded over $(s2, v3)$, since users requesting $(s2, v3)$ can be served by an alternative version $(s2, v2)$, which has a close bitrate to the originally requested one, and no version of segment $s1$ exists in the system.

In our design, $Y_{(s,v)}^{(T)}$ is calculated as the "mismatch" level of the bitrate if v is not transcoded as follows:

$$Y_{s,v}^{(T)} = \begin{cases} \min_w (B(v) - B(w))/B(v), & \exists w \in G^{(T)}(s), w < v \\ \gamma, & \text{otherwise} \end{cases},$$

where $G^{(T)}(s)$ is the set of all the versions of the segment existing in the system. When there is a lower-version replacement, a large $Y_{(s,v)}^{(T)}$ indicates that users will receive a highly mismatched bitrate if the version v is not transcoded, such that version v is important to segment s quality-wise. When there is no lower-version replacement, $Y_{(s,v)}^{(T)}$ is assigned with a large value γ, indicating that no replacement version of the segment has been transcoded.

Based on the definition of the importance level of segments, we determine which segments to be transcoded by formulating it as an optimization problem as follows:

$$\max_{\mathbf{E}^{(T)}} \sum_{(s,v) \in \mathbf{E}^{(T)}} e_{(s,v)}^{(T)}, \tag{5.2}$$

Fig. 5.9 Segment importance in the context of online transcoding

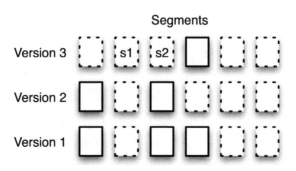

subject to:

$$\sum_{(s,v)\in\mathbf{E}^{(T)}} C(s,v) \leq \sum_{r} I^{(T)}(r),$$

where $\mathbf{E}^{(T)}$ is the set of segments to be transcoded in time slot T, $C(s,v)$ is the amount of computational resources required to transcode a segment (s,v), and $I^{(T)}(r)$ is the aggregated idle computational resources from the CDN region r. According to [9], it takes different amounts of CPU time to generate different segments in the same video. In our design, we use the average CPU time spent on generating historical segments of a particular version and size to estimate the computational resources required to transcode any segment with that version and size.

The rationale of the optimization that is also a 0–1 knapsack problem is to select a set of segments that are the most important ones in the next time slot T. We design the following algorithm to solve this problem: (1) we collect the information for prediction in a centralized manner, e.g., users (resp. backend servers) report which segments they are downloading (resp. the CPU load information) to a centralized server, which will perform the prediction; (2) based on the prediction, we rank the requested segments in descending order of $e^{(T)}_{(s,v)}/C(s,v)$; (3) we iteratively select segments from the ranked list to transcode and update the computational resource consumption until the available idle computational resources are used up.

5.4.3.2 Scheduling Transcoding Tasks Across Regions

After the tasks are selected, they are to be scheduled to different regions where backend servers can provide the computational resources. Without lose of generality, we use $A^{(T)}_{(s,v)}$ to denote the region where segment (s,v) will be transcoded—the segment will be replicated from this region which originally stores the transcoded version, to other regions where users request it.

According to our measurement studies in Sect. 5.3, heterogeneous preferences of video versions exist in different regions due to the different download speeds from the servers at different regions. As a result, it is promising to strategically assign transcoding tasks for different segments to backend servers at different CDN regions for a minimized replication cost.

We use $F[(s,v),r]$ to denote the overall replication cost if segment (s,v) is transcoded in region r. It can be calculated as follows:

$$F[(s,v),r] = \sum_{r'\neq r,\mathbf{J}^{(T)}_{(s,v),r'}>\beta} Z_{r,r'}(s,v),$$

where $\mathbf{J}^{(T)}_{(s,v),r'}$ is the number of requests of segment (s,v) to be served by a region r', $Z_{r,r'}(s,v)$ represents the replication cost when segment (s,v) is replicated from region r to region r', depending on the size of the segment and the bandwidth between CDN regions r and r' [6]. β is a threshold of the number of requesting users from a region to trigger a replication. $\mathbf{J}^{(T)}_{(s,v),r'}$ can be derived from the optimization in (5.1), which determines the redirection of users. The rationale of this definition is that in our design, a transcoded segment can be replicated from where it is transcoded to other regions where it is substantially requested (i.e., $\mathbf{J}^{(T)}_{(s,v),r'} > \beta$)—a large $F[(s,v),r]$ indicates a large replication cost between CDN regions if segment (s, v) is transcoded by region r. The task assignment problem is then formulated as follows:

$$\min_{A^{(T)}} \sum_{(s,v)\in\mathbf{E}^{(T)}} F[(s,v), A^{(T)}_{(s,v)}], \qquad (5.3)$$

subject to:

$$\sum_{(s,v)\in\mathbf{E}^{(T)}} C(s,v) \le I^{(T)}(r), \forall r \in \mathbf{R}.$$

The rationale of the optimization is to schedule the segment transcoding tasks to different CDN regions, such that the overall replication cost can be minimized. In our implementation, we also design a practical algorithm to heuristically solve the problem, as follows: (1) We first rank all the pairs of the CDN regions and segments (i.e., $|\mathbf{R}|\,|\mathbf{E}^{(T)}|$ elements), in ascending order of $F[(s,v),r]$; (2) we pick the region-segment pair "$r - (s, v)$" with the smallest $F[(s, v), r]$ and assign the transcoding task of segment (s, v) to region r; (3) we update the available computational resources of the selected region, and iteratively perform (2) until all computational resources in all regions are fully used up. This algorithm can be implemented in a centralized manner, where a central server is deployed to collect the request information from streaming servers and make the decisions. Such implementation has been well applied in peer-assisted on-demand streaming systems [8], where a central server tracks the storage status of peers to help them find each other.

In our design, regions with a request number of a segment larger than β will serve a replication of the segment, whereas for other regions with numbers of requests smaller than β, they will further redirect the users to other regions with the segment transcoded or replicated, according to the users' preferences.

5.5 Performance Evaluation

5.5.1 Experimental Setup

We develop an event-driven simulation platform which takes users' viewing activities, and the transcoding and redirection decisions as events to drive the experiments. We compare our design with a pre-transcoding baseline scheme. Details are as follows.

- *Users*. According to models summarized from user viewing traces in BesTV, we simulate 10,000 users, each of whom repeatedly joins different video sessions.

After a user joins the system, she selects a video to watch according to the video popularity distribution. The indices of the first segments users start to view also follow a zipf distribution, with a shape parameter 1.29. When playing a video, a user plays (downloads) sequentially the segments, and may jump to a rand segment ahead with a probability of 0.05. The rationale is that in a video session, how users request segments follow a pattern that users generally play forward and issue a few seeks, most of which are forward seeks [20]. Before leaving a video session, the number of segments a user downloads follows a zipf distribution with a shape parameter 1.12.

- *Video Provider.* New videos are published every 10,000 time slots. The popularity of videos follows a zipf distribution with a shape parameter 1.76. In our experiments, the default number of segments in each video is 200, and the default number of versions is 4, if not specified otherwise. The bitrates of the versions are uniformly distributed between the lowest user download speed, and the highest user download speed. The segment length is 10 s, and the computational resources required to transcode a segment is randomly distributed within [5, 10] CPU seconds [13].

- *CDN Regions.* We simulate 30 regions. We set a region-to-user average download speed according to the download speed of 10,000 IP prefixes randomly selected from the CDN traces, i.e., the download speed of an IP prefix is the average download speed of users with the same prefix in a one-week time span, varying from 70 Kbps to 2.2 Mbps. In our experiments, the aggregated CDN bandwidth is sufficient for all the users to stream at their ideal bitrates, and we randomly divide the bandwidth allocation across the regions. We assign the replication cost between each pair of regions within [0, 1], and a replication parameter $\beta = 10$. A region has a varying idle computational resources over time with CV randomly selected in [0, 0.5], and the average amount of computational resources will be presented in the experiments.

Baseline Algorithm. We compare our design with a general pre-transcoding and load-based redirection strategy: (1) for segment transcoding, all versions of the videos are transcoded before publication, and each transcoded segment is replicated to 3 initial regions randomly selected (i.e., the pre-transcoding scheme); (2) for user redirection, when requesting a segment, a user is redirected to a region which currently has the highest available upload bandwidth (i.e., the load-based redirection scheme).

5.5.2 Experimental Results

5.5.2.1 Computational Resources Saved

In this experiment, we assume that the CDN can provide unlimited computational resources when transcoding is performed, such that we can satisfy all the segment requests of users. In Fig. 5.10, the curves represent computational resources saved by

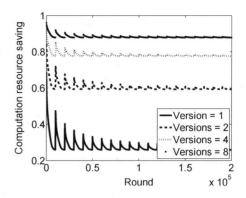

Fig. 5.10 Computational resources saved by online transcoding under different number of versions

our design under different number of versions, compared with the pre-transcoding scheme. In particular, each sample is the fraction of computational resources that has been saved over the computational resources required to transcode videos to all the versions till a simulation round. We observe that as the number of versions increases, the computational resources saved by online transcoding increases, e.g., more than 90% of the computational resources can be saved when the number of versions is greater than 8. The reason is that transcoding segments with no viewer to many versions costs a large amount of computational resources. We also observe that the amount of computational resources saving decreases in the first several rounds when new videos are published, and becomes stable afterwards. The reason is that in our design, computational resources is mainly used to transcode the most popular segments after the videos are published, and users who watch videos later largely request the segments that have already been transcoded.

Then, we investigate the impact of the number of videos published each time and the number of segments in each video. In this experiment, we fix the number of versions to 4. In Fig. 5.11, each bar represents the computational resources saved when a particular number of videos are published each time. We observe that publishing

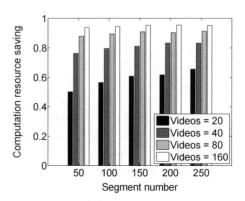

Fig. 5.11 Computational resources saved by online transcoding under different numbers of videos and segments

a large number of videos per time slot generally leads to larger amount of computational resources saved. The reason is that the popularity distribution of the videos is heavy-tailed, and more videos with no viewer cause more waste of computational resources with the pre-transcoding scheme.

5.5.2.2 Streaming Bitrates at Users

Taking advantage of online transcoding, users are redirected to their ideal regions to download the videos. We compare our redirection strategy with the load-based redirection scheme. In Fig. 5.12, each curve plots the average download speed achieved at users versus the rank of users. We observe that our strategy can effectively schedule users to their ideal regions, with an average 181 Kbps improvement of download bandwidth than the load-based redirection scheme. The reason is that the load-based redirection scheme only considers segment replication and available bandwidth of the regions, while our strategy allows users to choose their ideal regions.

Furthermore, we compare the best versions users receive under different redirection strategies. Again, we fix the number of versions to 4. As illustrated in Fig. 5.13, each curve represents the version downloaded versus the user rank. We observe that as many as 44.8% of the users receive a version of a higher bitrate with our strategy than that with the load-based redirection scheme. In particular, over 4.5x users receive the version with the highest bitrate with our redirection strategy than with the load-based redirection scheme.

5.5.2.3 Fitness of the Transcoded Segments

In the following experiment, we will evaluate the effectiveness of our transcoding task schedule, in how well the transcoded segments match the users' requests. We compare our transcoding scheduling scheme with an FIFO-based scheme, where the transcoding tasks are performed according to request arrivals in an FIFO

Fig. 5.12 Comparison of download speed achieved at users under different redirection strategies

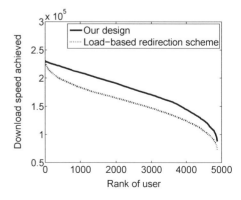

Fig. 5.13 Comparison of best versions achieved at users under different redirection strategies

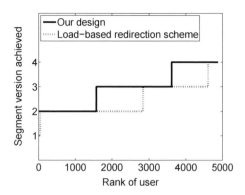

manner. For a fair comparison, we assume that users have already been redirected to regions according to our redirection strategy for both schemes. By varying the average computational resources in the regions, we evaluate the fitness of the transcoded segments. In Fig. 5.14, each sample represents the average bitrate difference between the bitrates of the received version and the requested version at all users versus the average computational resources of the region, calculated as the average number of segments that can be generated by the region. Note that the real computational resources may be different across the regions as it takes different amount of computational resources to transcode different versions. A larger difference indicates a larger streaming quality degradation, as users have to receive a replacement segment with a much smaller bitrate. We observe that the average bitrate difference is much smaller with our design. In particular, our strategy can reduce the number of users who have to receive a segment of a mismatched version by over 42.2%.

Fig. 5.14 Comparison of bitrate mismatch under different transcoding schedules

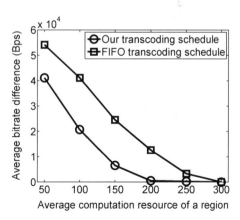

Fig. 5.15 Average replication cost per time slot versus the number of versions

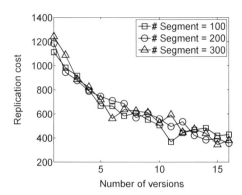

5.5.2.4 Replication Cost

Our design utilizes regional preferences of versions when assigning transcoding tasks. Next, we evaluate the replication cost under different numbers of video versions. In Fig. 5.15, each curve represents the replication cost versus the number of versions, with a particular number of segments in each video. We observe that a larger number of versions leads to a smaller replication cost. The reason is that when more versions are available, our design can effectively allow regions to transcode heterogeneous versions that best meet their users' demand. We also observe that the number of segments has little impact on the replication cost, implying that we can use a small amount of time for adaptive scheduling without incurring increased replication cost. As more and more versions are used in today's adaptive streaming systems, our design reduces not only the waste of computational resources for transcoding, but also the replication cost of the transcoded segments.

References

1. V.K. Adhikari et al., Unreeling netflix: understanding and improving multi-CDN movie delivery, in *IEEE International Conference on Distributed Computing Systems (INFOCOM)* (2012)
2. D. Antoniades et al., Available bandwidth measurement as simple as running wget, in *Passive and Active Measurement Conference (PAM)* (2006)
3. Bestv, http://www.bestv.com.cn/
4. A.J. Cahill, C.J Sreenan, An efficient CDN placement algorithm for the delivery of high-quality TV content, in *ACM International Conference on Multimedia (Multimedia)* (2004)
5. M. Cha et al., Analyzing the video popularity characteristics of large-scale user generated content systems. IEEE/ACM Trans. Netw. **17**(5), 1357–1370 (2009)
6. Y. Chen, R.H. Katz, J.D. Kubiatowicz, Dynamic replica placement for scalable content delivery, in *International Workshop on Peer-to- Peer Systems* (2002)
7. J. Cohen et al., Keeping track of 70,000+ servers: the akamai query system, in *Proceedings of the 24th international conference on Large installation system administration* (USENIX Association, 2010), pp. 1–13

8. Y. Huang et al., Challenges, design and analysis of a large-scale P2P-VoD system, in *ACM SIGCOMM* (2008) [9]
9. Z. Huang et al., CloudStream: delivering high-quality streaming videos through a cloud-based SVC proxy, in *IEEE International Conference on Distributed Computing Systems (INFOCOM)* (2011)
10. ISO/IEC JTC 1/SC 29/WG 11 (MPEG), Dynamic Adaptive Streaming Over HTTP (2010)
11. F. Lao, X. Zhang, Z. Guo, Parallelizing video transcoding using map-reduce-based cloud computing, in *IEEE International Symposium on Circuits and Systems* (2012)
12. Z. Li et al., Cloud transcoder: bridging the format and resolution gap between internet videos and mobile devices, in *ACM Network and Operating System Support for Digital Audio and Video (NOSSDAV)* (2012)
13. L. Liang, The cloud video material transfer code system design in the global station network environment, in *IEEE International Conference on Image Analysis and Signal Processing (IASP)* (2012), pp. 1–3
14. G. Peng, CDN: content distribution network, in *arXiv preprint cs/0411069* (2004)
15. T. Stockhammer, Dynamic adaptive streaming over HTTP: standards and design principles, in *ACM Conference on Multimedia Systems (MMSys)* (2011)
16. Tencent, http://www.tencent.com/
17. A. Vakali, G. Pallis, Content delivery networks: status and trends. IEEE Internet Comput. **7**(6), 68–74 (2003)
18. N. Wu et al., Streaming HD H.264 encoder on programmable processors, in *ACM International Conference on Multimedia (Multimedia)* (2009)
19. G. Peter Zhang, Time series forecasting using a hybrid ARIMA and neural network model. Neurocomputing **50**, 159–175 (2003)
20. C. Zheng, G. Shen, S. Li, Distributed prefetching scheme for random seek support in peer-to-peer streaming applications, in *ACM Workshop on Advances in Peer-to-Peer Multimedia Streaming* (2005)

Chapter 6
Concluding Remarks

We conclude the book as follows:

1. **To understand user preferences in online social video services**, it is important to use information from online social networks and online content sharing networks jointly to perform recommendations for user-generated content, i.e., recommending videos that users are likely to import or re-share in online social networks. We show how to use social propagation simulation and content similarity analysis to update the user-content matrix. Based on the user-content matrix update, it is common to construct a joint user-content space using social relation, content similarity and user activity to calculate the relevance between users and videos for preference inference. Such solutions have been verified in real-world systems including Weibo.

2. **To effectively allocate network resources in edge networks**, previous efforts have been devoted into the connections between information propagation and actual views in a video sharing site. Based on discoveries of the connections between online social networks and online video sharing systems, it is thus possible to predict video requests based on propagation patterns. A prediction framework using neural network structure has been explored to improve global-scale video service deployment. Real-world experiments show the potential of such prediction based network resource allocation in improving the efficiency of network resource allocation under highly churning content requests.

3. **To further deploy content over the edge networks,** the book presents a propagation-based social content delivery framework. There are unique propagation patterns that demonstrate social, geographical and temporal localities in the social propagation. Based on the propagation patterns, propagation predictors can be designed to enable propagation-based socially aware replication strategies to serve such social content to users. Three replication indices are proposed in this book: a geographic influence index, a global-audience index and a local-

© The Author(s) 2018
Z. Wang et al., *Online Social Media Content Delivery*,
SpringerBriefs in Computer Science, https://doi.org/10.1007/978-981-10-2774-1_6

audience index, which can guide the region selection, bandwidth reservation and cache replacement in the proposed joint edge-cloud and peer-assisted replication framework.

4. **To serve dynamic social video content,** joint transcoding and delivery has been investigated. A joint online transcoding and geo-distributed delivery strategy allows one to explore the new design space for adaptive video streaming. The book presents how to connect video transcoding and video delivery based on users' preferences for CDN regions and regional preferences of versions to transcode. Being aware of users' preferences of CDN regions, the design strategically performs user redirection such that videos can be streamed at high bitrates to the users. Taking into consideration the heterogeneous importance of segments and regional preferences for versions to transcode, the design carefully schedules the transcoding tasks such that segments are transcoded to satisfy users' demands in each region, with little need for cross-region replication. Optimization problems are formulated and efficiently solved to derive these strategies.

This book aims at improving the user experience in today's large-scale social multimedia services, in which applications are becoming user-aware, people are socially connected, content is dynamically generated and processed according to varying contexts, and information propagates in a cascading manner. By using measurement, optimization and system implementation as tools, this study has verified that the data-driven and socially aware design philosophy can be a very promising approach to advance the system performance and service quality in socialized multimedia services to the next level.

Index

© The Author(s) 2018
Z. Wang et al., *Online Social Media Content Delivery*,
SpringerBriefs in Computer Science, https://doi.org/10.1007/978-981-10-2774-1